TIMESAVER **FOR**

IELTS Practice Tests & Tips

(5.5–7.5)

By Liz Joiner

Contents

Practice Test 3

Practice Test 4

Introduction

Who is this book for?

This book is for teachers of students who are preparing for the Academic version of the IELTS test and require extra practice material for the four components of the test: Listening, Reading, Writing and Speaking. Ideal as a supplement to any IELTS or upper-intermediate / advanced coursebook, the book is suitable for students who are aiming at a level of 5.5 – 7.5 in the IELTS test.

The IELTS test: an overview

The International English Language Testing System (IELTS) is a test that measures the language proficiency of people who want to study or work in environments where English is used as a language of communication. An easy-to-use 9-band scale clearly identifies proficiency level, from non-user (band score 1) through to expert (band score 9).

IELTS is available in two test formats – Academic or General Training – and provides a valid and accurate assessment of the four language skills: listening, reading, writing and speaking. This Timesaver title focuses on the Academic version of the test.

There are four components to the Academic test.

Listening 30 minutes (plus 10 minutes for transferring answers)
There are four sections with 40 questions in total.

Reading 60 minutes
There are 40 questions based on three long passages, chosen to test a wide range of reading skills.

Writing 60 minutes
There are two writing tasks. For Task 1, students will be asked to describe, summarise or explain information presented in a graph, table, chart or diagram in a minimum of 150 words. For Task 2, students will be asked to write an essay giving an opinion, argument or solution to a problem in a minimum of 250 words.

Speaking 11–14 minutes.
There are three parts: interview, long turn and two-way discussion.

Scoring
Each component of the test is given a band score. The average of the four scores produces the overall band score. Candidates are not awarded a pass or fail – all candidates receive an IELTS test score.

The IELTS scale

BAND SCORE	SKILL LEVEL	DESCRIPTION
9	Expert user	The test taker has fully operational command of the language. Their use of English is appropriate, accurate and fluent, and shows complete understanding.
8	Very good user	The test taker has fully operational command of the language with only occasional unsystematic inaccuracies and inappropriate usage. They may misunderstand some things in unfamiliar situations. They handle complex and detailed argumentation well.
7	Good user	The test taker has operational command of the language, though with occasional inaccuracies, inappropriate usage and misunderstandings in some situations. They generally handle complex language well and understand detailed reasoning.
6	Competent user	The test taker has an effective command of the language despite some inaccuracies, inappropriate usage and misunderstandings. They can use and understand fairly complex language, particularly in familiar situations.
5	Modest user	The test taker has a partial command of the language and copes with overall meaning in most situations, although they are likely to make many mistakes. They should be able to handle basic communication in their own field.
4	Limited user	The test taker's basic competence is limited to familiar situations. They frequently show problems in understanding and expression. They are not able to use complex language.
3	Extremely limited user	The test taker conveys and understands only general meaning in very familiar situations. There are frequent breakdowns in communication.
2	Intermittent user	The test taker has great difficulty understanding spoken and written English.
1	Non-user	The test taker has no ability to use the language except a few isolated words.

For full details on the IELTS test, go to: **www.ielts.org**

How do I use this book?

This *Timesaver for Exams* contains two different types of material: twelve Boost Your Score skills lessons and four authentic Practice Tests.

Boost Your Score lessons

The twelve Boost Your Score lessons provide practice of common challenges which students face in the four parts of the test. These materials are designed to be used before a Practice Test to develop your students' exam strategies. Students can then go on to apply these skills in the Practice Test. Boost Your Score lessons offer focused practice of exam sub-skills, such as describing data (Writing) or recognising paraphrase (Reading), and practice of specific task types, e.g. multiple-choice tasks (Listening), or organising a discussion (Speaking). Alternatively, the Boost Your Score materials can be used as stand-alone exam-oriented skills lessons alongside your coursebook.

- Boost Your Score lessons are designed to be teacher-led with clear instructions on the pages, which are all photocopiable.

- The part of the test and the lesson focus are clearly labelled at the top of each lesson.

- This symbol (40 mins) indicates the approximate lesson length. (Please note that timings may vary according to class size and language level.)

- Boost your Score tips provide advice for exam strategy.

- The answer key gives full explanation of the answers.

- Some activities include pairwork to generate more language and encourage students to engage more fully with the task. These can be adapted depending on context and class size.

Practice Tests

This *Timesaver for Exams* provides four complete and authentic-level Practice Tests with answer key for all four components of the test. Depending on your students' needs, you can use the Practice Tests in this *Timesaver for Exams* to target particular parts of the test or to set up a mock test. The Practice Tests are annotated with 'Think it through' tips to provide support for students. The tips aim to help students identify and avoid common mistakes and to help them build strategies for exam success. Practice Test 4 contains less support in order to increase student autonomy and provide a more authentic exam experience.

How do I set up an authentic Listening Practice Test?

The complete Listening Practice Tests each take about forty minutes. Make photocopies of the Practice Test question sheets as well as the answer sheet on page 108 for each of your students. This symbol (🎧) indicates the relevant track on the accompanying CDs. For example, this symbol (🎧) indicates CD2, track 9. As in the exam, time is given on each recording for the students to read each question before they listen. Emphasise to your students the importance of using this time, particularly as the students will hear each recording only once. At the end of each of the four sections, allow students 30 seconds to check their answers. Once students have listened to all four recordings and checked their answers, give them ten minutes to copy their answers onto the answer sheet.

How important is exam strategy to exam success?

The Boost Your Score lessons and Practice Tests in this *Timesaver for Exams* will support teachers and help learners prepare adequately for the test. Familiarity with each part of the test is essential for students to be able to perform at their best. Practice of discrete test task types helps students to develop fundamental skills such as note-taking and listening or reading for relevant information. In addition, practice tests can help students prepare by giving them a chance to focus on maintaining concentration, time management and coping with anxiety. These skills are crucial for all IELTS students, whatever their level.

The Timesaver series

The Timesaver series provides hundreds of ready-made lessons for all language levels and age groups, covering skills work, language practice and cross-curricular and cross-cultural material. See the full range of print and digital resources at: **www.scholastic.co.uk/elt**

45 mins

How to ... listen for cues

1a   **Read sentences a–f and their paraphrases. <u>Underline</u> the paraphrase that matches the phrase in italics each time.**

Example: Some reference to scientific research *is recommended*.
<u>It would be preferable</u> if students referred to scientific research in their presentations.

a) A qualification in art is *essential* for this job.
In order to apply for the job all candidates are required to have an art degree.

b) The artist's ambitions were at first considered *unrealistic*.
Initially, everyone believed it unlikely that the artist would achieve her ambitions.

c) Pupils *are not allowed* on the school trip without a sunhat.
Participation in the school trip is not permitted for pupils who do not have a sunhat.

d) *A lack of* evidence meant that people didn't believe the professor's claims.
People weren't convinced by what the professor said as there simply wasn't enough evidence.

e) Full-time students *pay less* for bus tickets.
Bus travel is available at a greatly reduced price for those who study full time.

f) *A large part* of each lesson will be dedicated to speaking practice.
It is planned that speaking practice will make up a significant proportion of every lesson.

> **Boost your score!**
>
> Paraphrases are words and expressions with similar meaning. They are often used to cue the answers in the recording.

1b   **Choose four of the paraphrases you <u>underlined</u> and put each one in a new sentence.**

Example: <u>*required to have*</u>

In my country drivers are required to have their driving licences with them whenever they drive.

> **Boost your score!**
>
> In sentence and note completion tasks, you will need to listen for paraphrases of the notes on the question paper. The paraphrases will help to cue the answers.

2a   **Cues are words or expressions which tell you that the answer is coming.**

Example: *The language course begins on (i) ....*

The start date for the language course is Tuesday at 9 am.

cue

2b   🎧 **Listen to the following extracts, and use the listening cues to help you identify the answers. Write ONE WORD only in each gap.**

a) Professor Shaw worked with a .... to write her first textbook.

b) The college is near a ....

c) One well-known piece of art in the museum is made of ....

d) New technology has allowed more .... for most students.

e) Some students failed to find a .... which would have helped them complete their homework.

f) Pupils should submit a *proposal* before beginning their essay.

2c   📄 **Now look at the transcript on page 110 and <u>underline</u> the cue that comes before each of the answers.**

✎ EXAM TASK

3a 🎧 **Listen to a lecture about the work of sculptor, Anish Kapoor.**

*Write **ONE WORD ONLY** in each gap.*

1   Kapoor's sculptures are well-known for their eye-catching ....

2   Kapoor is originally from ....

3   One artwork with a .... surface is on display in Chicago.

4   In 2009, Kapoor created a work in the shape of a .... in New Zealand.

5   The red sculpture is made of .... and steel.

6   Kapoor worked with an .... to build a sculpture for the London Olympics.

7   A performance venue in Japan is unusual because it can be ....

8   A key feature of Kapoor's work is people's .... with it.

Orbit

> **Boost your score!**
>
> In sentence completion tasks, look at the words around the gap carefully before you listen. These will help you to identify the cues when you hear them.

Anish Kapoor

3b 📄 **Look at the transcript on page 110 and identify the cues for each answer. What examples of paraphrasing can you find?**

How to ... approach completion tasks

1   Look at the headline and introductory text about a plant. Now read the article once through and find out why this plant is significant. (Don't look up any unfamiliar vocabulary.)

2   Work in pairs and discuss the general argument of the article.

INVASIVE *pollen*

Ragweed gives off pollen that plays havoc with the human immune system

One of America's most irritating weeds threatens to spoil the summer months for thousands of Britons who are prone to crippling hay fever attacks. Ragweed has established a beachhead in central Europe and is spreading westwards towards Britain. A single ragweed plant can spew out a billion, highly allergenic pollen grains in just one season.

American ragweed has been present in Europe for about a century but it emerged as a seriously invasive plant species in Hungary during the 1990s. An increasing number of Europeans are showing signs of ragweed allergy as the plants spread from Hungary to the fields of Italy, Austria, France and more northerly regions bordering the English Channel. Scientists fear it might only be a matter of time before the common ragweed, *Ambrosia artemisiifolia*, gains a foothold in Britain where it could become an invasive species with the help of warmer summers, milder winters and the formidable reproductive powers of the plant itself.

A scientific conference in Vienna this week has been called to address the problems posed by the plant species, which spreads with frightening rapidity along roadside verges, railway lines and newly cleared land.

'Common ragweed is not an issue here in the UK – yet. As global temperatures rise we are seeing very rapid spread of this highly invasive plant and it may only be a matter of time before it appears in the UK,' said Dr Clare Goodess, of the Climatic Research Unit at the University of East Anglia.

Common ragweed, which grows to a height of about a metre, is particularly irritating to the human immune system, producing pollen grains that are highly allergenic. Warmer summers extend the pollen season and higher concentrations of carbon dioxide in the atmosphere have been shown to boost the production of ragweed pollen.

In the US, ragweed pollen is one of the most common causes of hay fever and asthmatic attacks – 75 per cent of Americans who are allergic to pollen are allergic to ragweed pollen. It can also travel long distances, being found 400 miles out to sea and two miles up in the atmosphere – although the highest concentrations are found close to where the plants flower in late summer.

The northern limit of ragweed in Europe is moving further north with climate change, according to Dr

Jonathan Storkey, a plant ecologist at Rothamsted Research in Harpenden, Hertfordshire. 'The English Channel won't be a barrier to it,' he said. 'The concern about ragweed centres on the health issue rather than the problem of its invasiveness. We have invasive plant species already but this species has pollen that is highly allergenic – it's bad news for hay fever sufferers.'

Like other types of hay fever allergies, ragweed symptoms include a runny nose, sneezing, puffy or irritated eyes, and a stuffy or itchy nose and throat. Because ragweed releases its pollen between late summer and the first autumn frosts, it can significantly extend the hay fever season.

Tests by European scientists published two years ago showed that up to 60 per cent of people in Hungary show allergic sensitivity to ragweed pollen. High rates of sensitivity were also found in Denmark, the Netherlands and Germany and about a quarter of those showing ragweed pollen allergy also had symptoms of asthma.

Professor Torsten Zuberbier, of the Charite University of Medicine in Berlin said that ragweed pollen sensitivity was currently affecting about 2.5 per cent of the wider European population, which is the current threshold for a 'high prevalence' allergy.

The University of East Anglia will use its climate models to assess how rapidly ragweed is likely to spread further north in Europe given that the plant requires a long, hot summer to produce its pollen. Ian Lake, a climate modeller at East Anglia, said: 'We will analyse the likely impact of changes in climate, land use and air pollution on pollen-induced allergy over the coming decades and devise adaptation and prevention strategies to minimise the impact on global health.'

3a Read the summary paragraph below. Does it include the same information you discussed?

Common ragweed is a very common plant in the USA which is not native to Europe. Ragweed thrives in the increased temperatures caused by global climate change. Scientists predict that the weed, which is now present in Central Europe, could soon reach the UK where the milder climate as well as the rapid reproduction for which the plant is notorious could mean it spreads swiftly. However, it is not the problem of the plant's invasive nature which is concerning scientists, but its potential impact on hay fever sufferers, since the plant is known to cause strong allergic reactions.

3b How would you describe the language that is used in the summary? Can you think of reasons for this?

4 Look at this information below. Find the same information in the summary paragraph. <u>Underline</u> the language features which are used to condense this information in the summary.

Example:
a) Ragweed thrives in increased temperatures. Increased temperatures are caused by global climate change.

   Ragweed thrives in the increased temperatures caused by global climate change.

b) The weed is now present in Central Europe. Scientists predict it could soon reach the UK. The milder climate in the UK could mean it spreads swiftly. It is also notorious for its rapid reproduction.

c) There is potential for an impact on people who suffer from hay fever and this is concerning scientists.

5 Read some more sentences summarising information from the article. What type of word is needed to fill each of the gaps? Find the section of the article where each piece of information is given. Can you find ONE WORD in the section which could be used to complete each gap?

a) Ragweed is an invasive plant capable of producing a huge quantity of pollen .... in a single year.

b) Scientists are concerned at the issues raised by the .... at which the plant is spreading on certain types of land.

c) Sneezing and irritated eyes are symptoms caused by ragweed in common with other .... of allergenic plants.

d) Ragweed pollen, which affects 75% of American hay fever sufferers, is produced late in the year, prolonging the hay fever ....

e) Researchers at the University of East Anglia are developing .... to reduce the health risks of pollen sensitivity.

6 Find synonyms in the sentences in exercise 5 for the following words or phrases.

a) itchy

b) release (pollen)

c) a non-native plant likely to cause environmental imbalance

d) speed

e) extend

f) people who are sensitive to plant pollen

g) causing an allergic reaction

h) the time of year when pollen is present

i) grow over a large area

j) have an impact on

k) just one

7 Look at the headline and introductory text. What do you think this passage is about?

8 Read the passage once through. How does the information in this passage differ from that in the previous passage?

GET READY FOR THE SNEEZING SEASON

Hay fever is on the rise

Hay fever is already the curse of summer for around a quarter of people in the UK, but a new report claims that by 2030 one in two people living in towns and cities could be suffering from the illness. According to Professor Jean Emberlin, director of the National Pollen and Aerobiology Unit at the University of Worcester, who wrote the Hay Fever Health Report commissioned by Kleenex, 39 per cent of the UK population could succumb to the condition by 2030, affecting as many as 32 million people.

Otherwise known as allergic rhinitis, hay fever is caused when the body's immune system overreacts to pollen, an otherwise harmless substance, producing histamines which in turn cause the symptoms that can plague sufferers throughout the summer months.

The symptoms of hay fever are very similar to those you get when you have a cold. The natural reaction is to sneeze, as the body tries to rid itself of the pollen. But if sneezing fails, the pollen causes an allergic reaction and releases histamines which inflame the lining of the throat, nose and eyes. This causes a runny nose, sore and itchy throat and eyes and even pain in the sinuses as they become congested by the increased mucus. As a result of these symptoms, sufferers can find it difficult to concentrate, and sleep patterns can be disturbed too.

Hay fever affects some people much more than others. It has long been seen as a young persons' illness – 38 per cent of UK teenagers suffer from it as opposed to 25 per cent of the general population – and young sufferers tend to grow out of it as they get older. But this situation may be changing as the condition is affecting greater numbers of sufferers in middle age or later. Scientists suggest development of symptoms in later life could be triggered by new allergens or an increased pollen load in the air.

According to Professor Emberlin, lifestyle choices play a huge part in our susceptibility to hay fever. She says city living is one of the main culprits, because lack of exercise, lack of sleep and stress can all exacerbate the symptoms. Professor Emberlin explained: 'If you are stressed, then your body will produce more of the stress hormone cortisol. This has all sorts of effects on the body, including on the immune system, so it will tend to make your hay fever symptoms worse.'

Urban lifestyles are just one factor. Air pollution from vehicle exhaust fumes also plays a significant part, both directly and indirectly. Professor Emberlin explains that certain pollutants will stop the body from ridding itself of the allergens as effectively as it normally would. She said: 'Nitrous oxides will slow down the beating of the cilia so that allergens will stay in the respiratory tract, and also certain air pollutants will affect the permeability of the membrane so they will leak into the lining of the respiratory tract more easily.'

The increased sunlight and dry hot summers resulting from climate change will affect our susceptibility to hay fever since photochemical smogs will become more frequent and intense, exacerbating pollution and hay fever. But increased pollution will not be the only consequence. According to a new study presented to the American Academy of Allergy, Asthma and Immunology, higher temperatures may lengthen the time pollen is produced for certain plants. Estelle Levin from the academy said: 'Longer pollen seasons and high levels of pollen certainly can exacerbate symptoms for people with allergic rhinitis (hay fever) and for those who previously had minimal symptoms.'

✏ EXAM TASK

Boost your score!

Remember: the exact word you use to fill each gap must appear in the passage. You should not change the form of the word to fit the gap.

9

Questions 1–5

Complete the summary below.

*Choose **NO MORE THAN TWO WORDS** from the passage for each answer.*

Hay fever, or allergic rhinitis, is on the increase in the UK, **1** _____ teenagers and older people alike. Hay fever is the body's allergic reaction to pollen, triggering the release of histamines by the **2** _____ which irritate the lining of the throat, nose and eyes. Symptoms include sneezing, itchy eyes and painful sinuses, which may also disrupt a person's concentration and **3** _____. The rising number of hay fever sufferers is being blamed on the increased pollen load in the atmosphere as well as **4** _____ air pollution, which aggravates the symptoms. Higher levels of sunlight and extreme summers brought on by climate change **5** _____ the pollen season for some plants.

How to ... describe data

1 **Look at the chart. Are the statements a–h true or false? Correct the false statements.**

Example: The chart gives details of car ownership in the UK.

False – The chart describes England and Wales.

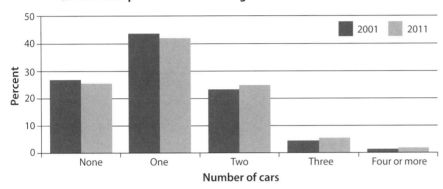

Car ownership in households in England and Wales in 2001 and 2011

a) The number of households without a car fell slightly from 2001 to 2011.

b) Approximately 25% of people did not have a car in 2011.

c) The number of households in England and Wales with three cars in 2001 was approximately 4 million.

d) The number of households with two cars rose steadily from 2001 to 2011.

e) Over the ten-year period, more households had no car than had two cars.

f) The majority of households choose to have one car, probably due to the high cost of running a car.

g) In 2011, two households in every hundred owned four or more cars.

h) The number of households with three cars is higher now than it was in 2001.

2   Look at these verbs which are used to describe trends and movements. Add the verbs from the box to the correct lists.

> climb   decline   decrease   drop   fall   fluctuate   grow
> increase   plateau   remain stable   remain steady   rise   waver

a   _go up_
....
....
....
....

b   _go down_
....
....
....
....

c   _stay at the same level_
....
....
....

d   _go up and down_
....
....
....

3   Work in pairs. <u>Underline</u> the verbs, adverbs and nouns that describe movement. In each group of sentences, which *two* have a similar meaning?

Example: **a)** There was <u>a sharp rise</u> in the cost of train travel. ✓
          b) The cost of train travel <u>rose significantly</u>. ✓
          c) There was <u>a minor rise</u> in the cost of train travel. ✗

1 **a)** The number of visitors to the museum increased slightly from 2001 to 2011.
   b) The number of visitors to the museum went up steeply in 2012.
   c) The number of visitors to the museum rose considerably in 2012.

2 **a)** The price of food increased steadily over the five-year period.
   b) The price of food increased dramatically over the five-year period.
   c) There was a gradual increase in the price of food over the five-year period.

3 **a)** There was a sudden drop in the number of adults working part-time.
   b) The number of adults working part-time plummeted.
   c) The number of adults working part-time dropped gradually.

4 **a)** Sales of goods fluctuated during the winter.
   b) Sales of goods remained steady throughout the winter.
   c) Sales of goods were stable in the winter period.

5 **a)** The number of complaints reached a high of twelve in January.
   b) The number of complaints peaked at twelve in January.
   c) The number of complaints grew to twelve in January.

Boost your score!

To achieve a band score of 7 or above for lexical resource, you need to describe data with precision. Using adverbs can help to express information more accurately and precisely. Using both verbs and nouns to describe trends and movement can demonstrate a variety of structures, improving your score for grammatical range and accuracy.

EXAM TASK

 Complete the exam task.

You should spend about 20 minutes on this task.

> *The table below gives information about the number of people in England who took part in five different sports once a week in 2005–2006 and 2015–2016.*
>
> *Summarise the information by selecting and reporting the main features, and make comparisons where relevant.*

Write at least 150 words.

Number of adults who took part in sports once a week in England 2005–2006 and 2015–2016

Sport	Participants 2005–2006 (millions)	Participants 2015–2016 (millions)
Swimming	3.2	2.5
Athletics	1.4	2.4
Cycling	1.7	2
Football	2	1.9
Golf	0.9	0.7

  Compare your answer with the model answer and answer the following questions.

a) Did you use any of the same verbs or adverbs?

b) Did you use a range of verb phrases and noun phrases to describe the data?

c) Did you include accurate information?

Boost your score!

If you have to describe data given as visual information, take the time to look at the data carefully.
- Read the title and check exactly what is described by the visual before you start.
- Look at vertical and horizontal axes in bar charts and graphs and check any labelling. Read the headings in tables carefully.
- Make sure you identify the units used to describe the data, e.g. percentages, thousands, millions.
- After you have finished the writing task, check your numbers are accurate.

90 mins

How to ... expand your answers

1 🎧 ¹/₃ **Listen to three candidates answering the following questions from the Speaking test, Part 1.**

   a) What do you like about the place where you live?

   b) How often do you go shopping?

   c) What was the last book that you read?

   Do they answer the questions well or not? Why? / Why not?

2a **Work in pairs. Write additional things you could talk about for each question.**

   a) *who I live with* ....

   ....

   b) ....

   ....

   c) ....

   ....

2b 🎧 ¹/₄ **Now listen to the candidates giving more extended answers. Tick any of the ideas that were on your list.**

2c 📄 **Look at the transcript on page 110 and check your answers.**

2d 🎧 ¹/₅ **Listen to another candidate answering question c. Does he answer the question well? Why? / Why not?**

> ### Boost your score!
>
> To achieve a band score of 7 or above you need to demonstrate that you can speak at length without losing coherence. It is important to give full answers to the questions and avoid short answers, even in Part 1. However, make sure everything you say is relevant to the question.

✏ EXAM TASK

3a   **Work in pairs.**

Student A	Student B
You are the examiner. Ask your partner the questions. If your partner gives a short answer, ask for more detail, e.g. *Why?* / *When?*	You are the candidate. Answer the questions below. Give full answers.

a) Can you describe the place where you live?

b) Do you like going shopping?

c) How often do you read a book?

d) Do you prefer studying alone or with other people?

e) What type of sports are popular in your country?

f) Are you good at cooking?

3b   **Swap roles and repeat.**

3c   **How well did your partner answer the questions? Give your partner some feedback.**

Boost your score!

Aim to give two or three reasons or examples in an answer. With an opinion question, try to see both sides of the argument, and give examples from both points of view.

4a   **Work in pairs. Answer the following questions from Part 3 of the Speaking test.**

a) How important is it for children to do sports at school?

b) Do you think it is good for children to play competitive sports and games?

4b   **Listen to a candidate discussing the same topics. Answer the questions below.**

a) What three reasons does she give for children doing sports at school?

b) Does she think it is good for children to take part in competitions? Why? / Why not?

4c   📄 **Look at the transcript on page 111 to check your answers.**

✏ EXAM TASK

5a   **Work in pairs. Ask and answer the following questions with full and detailed answers.**

a) What can schools do to encourage children to lead healthy lives?
(Give more than one idea each.)

b) Do you think all children should be taught to cook at school?
(Give reasons in favour and against.)

c) How can governments encourage people to lead healthy lifestyles?
(Think of at least two ideas each.)

d) Do you think people in your country generally lead healthy lifestyles?
(Give reasons to support your answer.)

5b   **Give your partner some feedback. How well did they answer the questions? Did they follow the instructions in brackets above? How could they improve their answers?**

LISTENING

 **SECTION 1**

Questions 1–5

Complete the notes below.

Write ONE WORD AND/OR A NUMBER for each answer.

Language School Information

> *Example*
>
> The school administrator is called (**0**) .... *Steven* ....

date

English class

July × —

All the next courses begin in **1** .... *September* ....

There are language classes on **2** .... *Tuesday* .... and
Friday mornings.

The teacher's name is Mrs **3** .... *Reade* ....

New students should bring a **4** .... *Photo* ....

The phone number to call about other courses is

5 .... *573-992* ....

> 💡 The answer to question 3 is a name – it must be spelled correctly to get a mark.

Questions 6–10

Complete the sentences below.

Write ONE WORD AND/OR A NUMBER for each answer.

Wed

Social activities

Every Friday there is a **6** .... *Party* .... for students.

The trip to London costs **7** .... *40 pounds* ....

Students will go sightseeing and visit a **8** .... *museum* ....

Film club takes place at the **9** .... *for local Library* ....

Plu

Students can find information about current events

in the **10** .... *cafe* ....

(10)

> 💡 What kind of social events can you think of?

> 💡 Listen for a place where a film club could take place.

 SECTION 2

Questions 11–15

Label the map below.

*Write the correct letter, **A–G**, next to Questions 11–15.*

Map of Morbourne Holiday resort

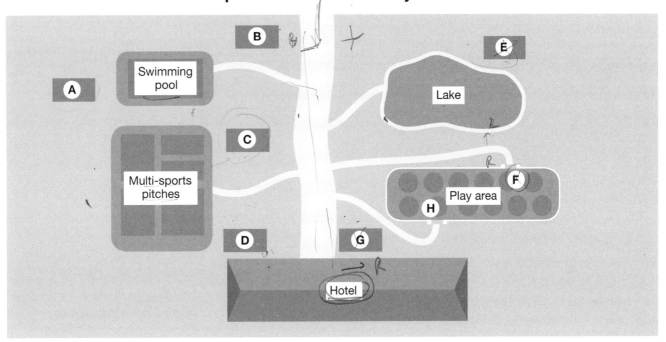

11	beauty spa	F	**14**	kids club D
12	outdoor fitness class	G / A (A)	**15**	souvenir shop B
13	bike hire	E		

Questions 16–20

Complete the sentences below.

*Write **NO MORE THAN TWO WORDS AND/OR A NUMBER** for each answer.*

16 The **quickest** way to get to the town centre is by ...Bus...

> Which types of transport might be quick?

17 **All** rooms have great views of the ...mountains...

18 ...Tea... is available for a small fee.

> Remember the answer must apply to **all** rooms.

19 The average temperature for this time of year is ...26X... degrees Celsius.

20 Meet at 10:15 tomorrow for a ...Hike...

🎧 SECTION 3

Questions 21–25

*Choose the correct letter, **A**, **B** or **C**.*

Course in Art Conservation

21 What **made Peter consider** a course in Art Conservation?

    A   a relative thought he would enjoy it

    B   a classmate said he would be good at it

    C   a teacher advised him it would help his future prospects

> 💡 The options in **A**, **B** and **C** may all be mentioned, but listen for the one that 'made Peter consider' the course.

22 What did a museum worker say was the best part of the job?

    A   working with interesting people

    B   continuing to learn new things

    C   feeling connected with future generations

23 Peter's tutor recommends that Peter improves

    A   his understanding of science.

    B   his organisational skills.

    C   his knowledge of art history.

24 What **surprised** Peter about the work when he volunteered at a gallery?

    A   the level of fitness that was needed

    B   the amount of report writing that he had to do

    C   the opportunities for ongoing training

> 💡 You will not hear the word 'surprised' in the recording — what other expressions could Peter use to talk about being surprised?

25 In the next month, Peter is looking forward to

    A   making a trip to a famous museum.

    B   starting his own conservation project.

    C   meeting an expert in art conservation.

Questions 26–30

What description do Pete and his tutor give of each of the following workshops?

*Choose **FIVE** answers from the box and write the correct letter, **A–G**, next to Questions 26–30.*

Descriptions
A   very different to other courses
B   popular with students ✓
C   highly specialised ✗
D   taught by experienced workers ✓
E   academically demanding
F   having some options for students
G   easy to apply practically

 How could the qualities be paraphrased? e.g. **A** very different – unusual / not the same

Courses

26   ceramics .... A ≠ A ....

27   paintings .... C B ....

28   frames .... D ....

29   sculptures ...... F .... (4)

30   paper ...... G ....

 You will hear each recording only ONCE. Use the time before the recording starts to read quickly through the questions, so that you are ready to listen for the relevant information.

 **SECTION 4**

Questions 31–40

Complete the notes below.

*Write **ONE WORD ONLY** for each answer.*

A young inventor

Peyton got the idea for his invention when he heard a report about **a 31** ....

> Notice the answer comes after 'a' – make sure the answer fits with this.

Salt water

- causes damage when it comes into contact with **32** .... and concrete

- causes long lasting problems for **33** .... systems

Building **34** .... is an effective way to prevent flooding in high risk locations

Sandbags

- **Advantages** – they are **35** .... and easy to make

> How can you paraphrase 'advantage'?

- Disadvantage – heavy

Improvements to polymer bags

- addition of salt meant polymer couldn't **36** .... sufficiently

- made adjustments to bags so they could be **37** ....

Competition

- got to work with a **38** ....

- **won** money and a **39** ....

> What is a typical competition prize, apart from money?

Now looking at a way to protect **40** ....

Make a photocopy of the Reading test answer sheet on page 109.

READING PASSAGE 1

*You should spend about 20 minutes on **Questions 1–14**, which are based on Reading Passage 1 below.*

The History of Jenolan Caves

Jenolan Caves in New South Wales are generally regarded as Australia's most remarkable cave system, with pure underground rivers and limestone crystal formations.

For thousands of years Jenolan Caves were known to the local Aboriginal people as *Binoomea* or 'Dark places'. Europeans did not come to the area until 1838; the first officially recorded discovery was by a local pastoralist called James Whalan. However, as local rumour would have it, the first European to find the caves was James McKeown, an ex-convict who is said to to have been using the caves as a place to hide. After 1838, James Whalan and his brother Charles discovered several openings, including the Elder cave in 1848. In 1860, the largest of the current caves on show: the Lucas cave, was discovered by Nicholas Irwin and George Whiting. The caves did not come under the direct control of the government until 1866 and the Aboriginal word *Jenolan* (meaning 'high mountain') was not formally adopted by the government until 1884.

In spite of this government control, the caves had little protection at first. In the early years, visitors freely broke rock formations and took pieces away from the caves as souvenirs. Damage is still visible in some caves today. Thanks primarily to the efforts of John Lucas, the local member of Parliament, this practice became illegal in 1872. The Lucas Cave was named after him, as recognition of his role in preserving this fragile location.

In the 1880s, Jenolan Caves emerged as a popular place for tourists. More exploration had occurred; for instance the caver Jeremiah Wilson had explored right to the end of the Elder Cave. In 1879 he had come across the Imperial Cave upon descending a shaft and this was followed by his discovery of the Left Imperial cave in 1880. This latter cave was renamed the Chifley Cave many years later in 1952, after the Australian Prime Minister, J.B. Chifley. Development began at this time; pathways were put in, provision was made for the protection of crystal formations and a house was constructed as accommodation for visitors. Wilson continued exploring, finding the Jersey Cave in 1891 and the impressive Jubilee Cave in 1893. The original buildings at the caves was partially destroyed by fire in 1898 and the present-day hotel (known as Caves House) was constructed.

By the year 1900, Jenolan was thriving as a tourist destination. However, there was still more to discover. In 1903, James Carvosso Wiburd became the Superintendent of Caves, and embarked upon one of the Jenolan's most successful periods of exploration. Whereas Wilson had focussed his exploration in the northern limestone, Wiburd forged deeper into the caves, south of the Grand Arch. The River and Pool of Cerberus Caves were first found by Wiburd in 1903, along with a further three caves in 1904. These discoveries elevated the status of Jenolan Caves worldwide, especially when the River (1904), Temple of Baal (1909) and Orient (1917) opened as show caves. Even after that time, the guiding staff continued to go into unchartered territory in the cave system and guides Ron Newbould and John Culley first found the Barralong Cave in 1963.

Lighting was an aspect of cave development that evolved over time. The first cave explorers carried candles, with spares and plenty of matches. However, a strong breeze could put out the flame; candle wax could spill on clothes and crystals, or a candle could be dropped into the water, leaving people stranded in the dark. Jeremiah Wilson fashioned candle holders that had a dish to catch the dripping wax and a spring-loaded device pushed the melting candle up through the burn hole, so that the flame continued to burn. The magnesium lamp came as an improvement on candles; this consisted of a clockwork mechanism which wound a burning wire into a wide reflector dish. In this way, cave features were individually illuminated. In 1887 came another innovation, electric searchlights, said to have the illuminating power of 120 candles.

Lieutenant Colonel E.C. Cracknell, Superintendent of Telegraphs, chose to light a chamber, at the top of the present-day stairs to the Chifley Cave using electric lighting. This cave was selected as it had the highest concentration of crystal features in any of the caves that had been discovered up to that point in time. The 18-metre climb meant 18 zinc and cast iron cell batteries had to be dragged up to the cave. Electricity allowed the caves to be seen to greater advantage and also prevented them from being discoloured by candle smoke.

Coloured lights were used to showcase some of the caves for the visit of the Governor of New South Wales in January 1893, beginning a tradition that was upheld for years thereafter. Some visitors remember these coloured lights appreciatively, but others prefer to view the caves in more natural lighting.

Today, Jenolan attracts over 230,000 annual visitors, who come to view the eleven show caves or even to try adventure caving. The question remains as to how many caves there are yet to be discovered.

Questions 1–7

Do the following statements agree with the Information given in Reading Passage 1?

In boxes 1–7 on your answer sheet, write

TRUE	if the statement agrees with the information
FALSE	if the statement contradicts the information
NOT GIVEN	if there is no information on this

1   There is doubt that James Whalan was the first European to discover the caves.

2   'Jenolan' was officially used as the name of the caves prior to 1884.

3   Before rules came into force in 1872, some visitors wrote on the walls of the caves.

4   The Chifley Cave was formerly known as the Imperial Cave.

5   Fire-resistant materials were used in the building of the Caves House.

6   Wiburd discovered a cave that was later opened to the public.

7   People who were employed as guides made discoveries of new caves.

Questions 8–11

Complete the notes below.

*Choose **ONE WORD ONLY** from the passage for each answer.*

Write your answers in boxes 8–11 on your answer sheet.

THINK IT THROUGH

In **note completion** tasks, the answers come in the same order as they do in the passage. Use the headings to help you find your place in the text.

For example, for question 8, you will find the answer in the passage after the information on candles. For question 10, you need to supply the heading – the answer for this will come between the information on *Magnesium lamps* and *Electric lighting* in the passage.

Lighting the Jenolan Caves

- **Candles**
    - could be extinguished by a **8** ....
    - wax could damage clothing and crystals

- **Magnesium lamps**
    - allowed **9** .... of the cave to be lit separately

- **10** ....
    - run on electricity
    - generated light equal to over a hundred candles

- **Electric lighting**
    - brought in by Cracknell
    - heavy **11** .... had to be taken up to the chamber
    - avoided damage caused by candles

Questions 12–14

Label the diagram below.

*Choose **NO MORE THAN TWO WORDS** from the passage for each answer.*

Write your answers in boxes 12–14 on your answer sheet.

A magnesium lamp

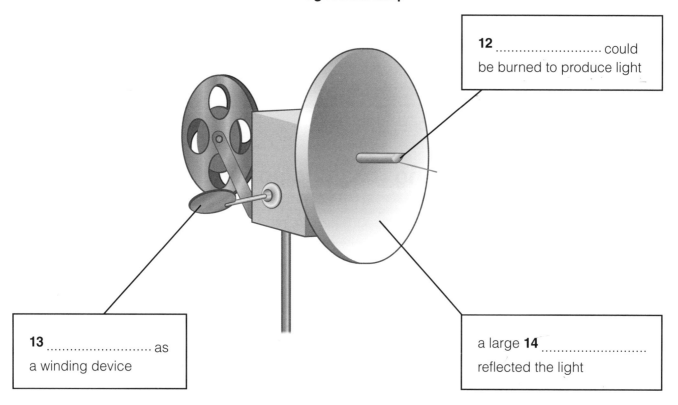

12 .... could be burned to produce light

13 .... as a winding device

a large **14** .... reflected the light

THINK IT THROUGH

What kind of information might fit in each of the gaps? Think about what part of speech should be used each time. Now go back to the part in the passage about magnesium lamps to find the actual words.

READING PASSAGE 2

You should spend about 20 minutes on **Questions 15–27**, *which are based on Reading Passage 2 below.*

Chimps and humans: how different are we?

Researchers are observing that chimpanzees show many similar behaviours to those of human beings – but how similar are chimps and humans really?

A   A chimp called Santino in Furuvik Zoo in Sweden has been found to be capable of planning ahead of time by calmly building up a pile of stones in the early morning hours ready for opening time when he would then hurl them at visitors. According to scientist Mathias Osvath of Lund University, Santino's behaviour shows that our fellow apes think in a very complex way.

'It implies that they have a highly developed consciousness, including life-like mental simulations of potential events,' Dr Osvath said. 'They most probably have an 'inner world' like we have when reviewing past episodes of our lives or thinking of days to come. When wild chimps collect stones or go out to war, they probably plan this in advance. I would guess they plan much of their everyday behaviour.' This is not the behaviour we come to expect of 'dumb' animals.

B   There are several different observations that point to chimps having a human-like nature. For instance, the hand gestures of chimps – such as the open-palm begging posture – are similar to those of humans and might derive from a common origin. Wild chimps have also been found to engage in a form of primitive warfare against neighbouring chimps. As well as these voluntary actions, they also experience infectious yawning, when one yawning member of a group sets off yawning in everyone else.

C   Chimps can be trained to accomplish 'human' challenges. A female chimp called Ai, for instance, was taught to count to ten and to remember five-figure numbers, just two short of the seven-digit telephone numbers most people can recall. Another chimp called Panbanisha had been trained to understand simple English sentences, although this fell short of being able to communicate in a true spoken language. The chimp was brought up to remember a lexigram, a computer screen full of symbols which she can press to produce a rudimentary response to a human voice. Panbanisha became able to recognise certain favourite or key words, such as 'outdoors' and 'M&Ms', when spoken in the proper context with a certain intonation.

D   Of course animals kept domestically can be trained to perform a wide variety of seemingly clever tricks, although there is mounting evidence that wild chimps have a more sophisticated understanding of the world than scientists once gave them credit for. Take, for example, the use of tools, which was once considered to be a defining feature of humanity. Wild chimps are now known to use tools, such as the use of sticks to 'fish' for termites or stones to crack open hard nuts. Indeed, a few years ago scientists filmed chimps using a 'tool kit' to fish for termites. They would create a hole in a termite nest with one, thick stick and push another, thinner stick with a deliberately frayed end down the same hole to catch the termites. This was the first known example of chimps using two different tools to perform a given task.

E   If culture is defined as passing on learning and customs to future generations, then chimps have it. Ten years ago, scientists published a large study drawing on a knowledge of more than 150 years of chimpanzee observations in the forests of central Africa showing that wild chimps have an array of behaviours that they pass on to their offspring. The scientist showed that while there were several examples of chimp behaviour, such as drumming on trees, that were shared across the entire region, there were many other examples – about 40 in total – that had evolved separately in different areas of the region and been handed on to subsequent generations inhabiting that area.

The chimps in Gombe national park in Tanzania, for instance, would fish for ants using a long branch which they would regularly swipe with their hands to collect the insects into a ball that they would put into their mouths. The chimps at other sites, meanwhile, would fish with shorter twigs that they would lick with their lips and tongues – a far more inefficient method. Scientists said that the difference came down to cultural practice passed on down the generations of geographically separated troupes of chimps.

F   While humans and chimps are close in terms of their genes, brain size is probably the most important distinguishing physical feature. The human brain is about three times larger than the brain of chimps in relation to body size. It is this immense growth of the human brain during the few million years of evolutionary history that really sets the two species apart and determines the uniquely human traits such as language, consciousness and creativity.

Humans also walk on two legs, whereas chimps have gone down the less-efficient knuckle-walking path. Bipedalism has freed our hands for using tools and allowed us to move large distances over open savannah, rather than being confined to forested areas. More sophisticated tools and their mastery of fire have enabled humans to exploit a different, more nutritious diet than chimps. So, while chimps are more closely related to humans than they are to other apes like gorillas, they are a nevertheless a distinct species of animal separated by millions of years of evolution.

Questions 15–20

Reading Passage 2 has six sections, **A–F**.

Which section contains the following information?

*Write the correct letter, **A–F**, in boxes 15–20 on your answer sheet.*

15   a list of characteristics which humans and chimps share *B*

16   details of a behaviour that was once considered to be exclusively human *D*

17   a reference to chimps passing on traditions to younger group members *E*

18   an example of a chimp that prepares for the future *A*

19   a reference to the greatest difference between chimps and humans *F*

20   examples of chimps that were taught to comprehend words *C*

Questions 21 and 22

*Choose **TWO** letters, **A–E**.*

Write the correct letters in boxes 21 and 22 on your answer sheet.

Which aspects of chimps' behaviour does the writer mention in order to show their similarity to humans?

A   showing hostility towards visitors ✓

B   fighting with others that live nearby ✓

C   memorising people's names

D   beating a rhythm with a stick

E   using a combination of implements to complete a task

THINK IT THROUGH

5-option multiple choice

Read the stem of the question carefully and underline the key words, e.g. 'Which aspects of <u>chimps' behaviour</u> does the writer mention in order to show their <u>similarity to humans</u>?' It is not enough that the behaviour in the options is mentioned in the passage – it must be mentioned for the purpose of showing similarity to human behaviour. For example, option **A** ('showing hostility towards visitors') is mentioned in the first section (Santino hurls stones at visitors). However, hostility is not the point of similarity – the writer actually uses this as an example of how both chimps and humans plan in advance.

Questions 23–27

Complete the summary below.

*Choose **ONE WORD ONLY** from the passage for each answer.*

Write your answers in boxes 23–27 on your answer sheet.

A distinct species

There are several respects in which chimps and humans differ. Humans have a greater ability to use

23 .... as they do not walk on their hands as chimps do. Humans can travel on different

terrain and longer **24** .... Furthermore, the human ability to control **25** .... ,

along with the use of more complex tools, is not shared by chimps. Thus, humans have a healthier

26 .... than chimps. Although it is true that chimps have less in common with

27 .... than with humans, they are still very different from people in many ways.

THINK IT THROUGH

Summary completion

Some summaries cover information from the whole passage but, more frequently, summary tasks are located in one part of the passage.

Use headings and the first sentence of the summary to help you find the relevant part of the passage. In this case, the heading (*A distinct species*) and first sentence let us know that we need to find part of the passage that focuses on the **differences** between chimps and humans. This comes in the final paragraph – words in the passage that point to differences include *whereas, rather than, different, while* and *distinct*.

READING PASSAGE 3

You should spend about 20 minutes on **Questions 28–40**, *which are based on Reading Passage 3 below.*

Graffiti

The role of graffiti in the city is exemplified by Zevs' *Dirty City Wall* in Copenhagen

We are accustomed to the idea of authorised art, commissioned and sanctioned by religious institutions, the state or that private individual with the deep pocket. Such art is entirely under the command of the poker-faced man with the serious purse. This is the story behind the marvels of the Renaissance and the years thereafter. In his oil sketches, you can see how Rubens danced to the not-so-delicate tunes of his patrons, aggrandising a donor here, bringing down others at times.

Street art, on the other hand, is paid for by no one, and it is not for re-sale in the marketplace. It often comes into being thanks to some nocturnal daredevil with a taste for what is often regarded as criminal behaviour. This is art made on the run. The studio is the artist's pocket. The canvas on which they work is entirely unprimed and unready for their assault. The fact that it is at odds with the authorities means that art of this kind often feels hectic in mood, hasty in execution, urgently political in its impulses, and prepared for the fact that it may disappear again just as rapidly as it has appeared because those who see it may regard it as an offence to the eye.

Such art has an air of wild chancing about it. It hits out at consumerism, greed, hypocrisy and the money-fuelled chattering of the art establishment. In a world at the visual mercy of corporate branding, street artists such as Ron English, for example, re-make brand images. His is an art of disruption and violation, an art which exists to do harm to the seductive global culture of corporate advertising.

The best of graffiti art, such as that of the French graffiti artist and "urban guerilla' Zevs, often plays with ideas of danger and prohibition. It seems to laugh at what gives offence to those who dislike it so much. Zevs produces some of his work with the aid of a high-pressure jet. Recently, he applied this technique to clean a stretch of unlovely, unacknowledged urban brick wall in Copenhagen, Denmark in such a way that what emerges from a century's accretion of grime and pollution was an image of wave upon wave of destructively engulfing flames, of which just fragments are shown in photographs. (This can be one of the problems with capturing street art with the camera: it is often difficult to contain on the page of a newspaper.) No one was ever burnt by a photo of a fire. Can you deface a building by cleaning it? Surely not. And yet some sort of violence has surely been done to its surface.

Zevs worked with the grain of what existed, the uneven surface of a red brick wall, and what such a material seemed to evoke – the wall of a factory building or terraced housing in a poor district. The modulation of tones – black, ochre, red, yellow and many points in between – was replicated in the flames themselves, which seemed to emerge from the wall as if they were some spiritual embodiment of its essential nature. This ghostly lashing of flames suggests the vanished power of industry. This unexpected depiction of flames on the side of the building also felt like a heartfelt expression of the fundamental energies of art beyond the tamed space of the gallery, art which had the freedom to be and to do whatever it wished at a moment of its own choosing.

What is more, it had no definable, containable dimensions. It could go on and on. It had no beginning and no end. It took possession, appropriated this section of wall in defiance of its original relatively humdrum purpose, which was nothing other than to be a wall, that which kept something in and that which kept something out. It became both a wall and a space of decorative ardour, engulfed by a fleeting image. We rather wish it to go on and on.

Zevs has disrupted many civic spaces in Europe and elsewhere. His projects have included the 'liquidating' of famous brand logos by re-painting them and allowing the paint to drip, thus creating the illusion that the logo is melting. In July, 2009, he was arrested in Hong Kong after a logo on the facade of a building was given such a makeover.

Questions 28–31

*Choose the correct letter, **A**, **B**, **C** or **D**.*

Write the correct letter in boxes 28–31 on your answer sheet

THINK IT THROUGH

When you are looking at the multiple-choice options, you may be able to predict what will come next. Then look for this answer in the options below. If you find the answer you expected, go back and double-check that it is in the passage. Also check options you believe are incorrect.

28 What point does the writer make in the first paragraph?

   A   The quality of art can depend on how much sponsors are willing to pay.

   B   Society is used to art that is controlled by people other than the artist.

   C   The Renaissance was a time when there was more artistic freedom.

   D   True artists should not be influenced by those that give them money.

29 What does the writer say about graffiti artists in the second paragraph?

   A   Their work depends on the funds available.

   B   Their work is deliberately offensive.

   C   They are physically fit.

   D   They are risk takers.

30 According to the writer, why does graffiti look a certain way?

   A   It has to be done quickly.

   B   It is designed to annoy people.

   C   It is produced by artists who have no training.

   D   It requires a lot of preparation in advance.

31 The writer mentions Ron English in order to

   A   prove that street artists can be commercially successful.

   B   show that graffiti artists tend to rebel against big business.

   C   argue that street artists need to promote their work.

   D   give an example of an artist who is sponsored by large companies.

Questions 32–37

Do the following statements agree with the views of the writer in Reading Passage 3?

In boxes 32–37 on your answer sheet, write

> **YES**   *if the statement agrees with the claims of the writer*
> **NO**   *if the statement contradicts the claims of the writer*
> **NOT GIVEN**   *if it is impossible to say what the writer thinks about this*

32   Removing dirt from the surface of a building was a type of attack.

33   Zevs' design in Copenhagen exploited the appearance of the wall that was already there.

34   Zevs' design in Copenhagen shows the growing influence of large corporations.

35   Zevs has exhibited some of his work in art galleries.

36   The wall Zevs used in Copenhagen formerly had a special function.

37   Zevs changes **the symbols used by well-known companies**.

> Which phrase in the passage do the words in bold paraphrase?

Questions 38–40

Complete the summary using the list of words, **A–G**, below.

Write the correct letters, **A–G**, in boxes 38–40 on your answer sheet.

Zevs: the 'urban guerilla'

The French artist Zevs is interested in concepts that are risky or **38** .... His work appears to find **39** .... in things that other people object to. As is the case with many pieces of street art, it was challenging for the true appearance of his work in Copenhagen to be conveyed in **40** .... in the newspaper.

A	beauty	**B**	unpopular	**C**	images
D	forbidden	**E**	humour	**F**	detail
G	words				

THINK IT THROUGH

In this type of summary, you need to choose words from the box below, rather than finding them in the passage. Sometimes the words may also appear in the passage but very often they will not. Instead, these words in the box will paraphrase or use synonyms for words in the passage (e.g. 'photographs', 'capturing with the camera' in the passage and 'images' in option **C**).

WRITING

TASK 1

You should spend about 20 minutes on this task.

> *The graphs below give information about money spent on online purchases in the USA from 2010, and the percentage of products purchased online in one company in the USA from 2007 to 2013.*
>
> *Summarise the information by selecting and reporting the main features, and make comparisons where relevant.*

Write at least 150 words.

 THINK IT THROUGH

Look carefully at the labelling on the two graphs. Both graphs show years along the horizontal axes, but what information and units are shown on the vertical axes?

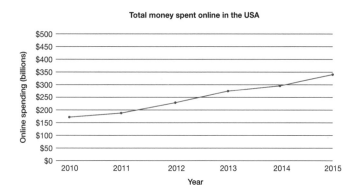

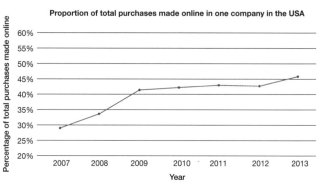

TASK 2

You should spend about 40 minutes on this task.

Write about the following topic:

> *Cars should be banned from city centres in order to reduce air pollution.*
>
> *Do you agree or disagree?*

Give reasons for your answer and include any relevant examples from your own knowledge or experience.

Write at least 250 words.

 THINK IT THROUGH

Decide what your opinion about the topic is before you start, and use arguments and examples to clearly support this opinion throughout the essay.

SPEAKING

PART 1: Introduction and interview

Sports

- Do you enjoy playing any sports? Why? / Why not?

- Did you do more or less sport when you were a child? Why? / Why not?

- Do you think it is important for all children to play sports at school? Why? / Why not?

- Are there any sports that you would like to try in the future? Why?

PART 2: Individual long turn

You will have to talk about the topic for one to two minutes.

You have one minute to think about what you are going to say.

You can make notes to help you if you wish.

> Talk about a **time** when you were late for something.
> You should say
>
> > what you were late for
> >
> > why you were late
> >
> > who was waiting for you
>
> and describe how you felt about being late.

Think of one occasion when you were late. If you run out of ideas before two minutes is up, don't start introducing new examples of being late, but add further detail to your story.

Final question

Are you often late for events?

PART 3: Two-way discussion

Being on time

How important is it to be on time in your country? Why?

What can people do to make sure they are on time for important events?

Politeness

Is it as important to be polite nowadays as it was in the past? Why? / Why not?

What are some of the things that people can do to show respect for others, apart from being on time? Why?

What are the best ways to teach children to behave with respect? Why?

Aim to make two or three suggestions here. In Part 3 of the test, you should be involved in a discussion rather than giving short answers to questions. Take advantage of this opportunity to show the range of your vocabulary and grammar knowledge.

How to ... choose multiple-choice answers

1a 🎧 1/14 **Listen and tick the methods of transport which are discussed.**

> bicycle   train   bus   car   taxi   coach   tram   ferry

1b 🎧 1/15 **The following task is from Section 2 of the Listening test. Listen and choose the correct answer, A, B or C.**

Visiting the city of Selwyn Springs

1   Which method of transport is it recommended to take to the beach?
   A   car
   B   train
   C   bicycle

2   Which method of transport is the most popular with parents of young children?
   A   bus
   B   taxi
   C   tram

3   Which method of transport offers less expensive tickets at certain times of day?
   A   coach
   B   ferry
   C   train

1c 📄 **Look at the transcript on pages 115 and 116. For question 1, the phrases that give the listener the correct answer are <u>underlined</u>, and the phrases which are distractors are circled.**

Example: **1** *'If you're staying here for a week or more, there are some excellent places to visit. We would strongly recommend going along to the bike hire point and taking the brand new* cycle path to the museum, *where you can easily spend a day looking round. The beach is of course an essential destination for visitors, and don't forget the* stunning river and waterfall, *which has lovely views.* <u>You'll ideally need a car to get to the coast,</u> *while* the river is accessible by rail *from the central station.'*

1d **Now underline the answer and circle the distractors for questions 2 and 3.**

2 *This area is popular with young people, families and the older generation alike, as there is a lot for people of every age to do here. For those of you who have come with your children, you'll find it easy to get around the city. Our local taxi drivers are friendly and efficient, and the city buses are easy to use. Most families with little ones tend to prefer the trams to get around though, as they are spacious, clean and welcoming to all.*

3 *You might fancy going slightly further afield, and taking a trip out of the city. If that's the case, look out for special offers on tickets, particularly if you can be flexible about when you go. The main coach company in this area has recently started running cheap deals if you travel before ten in the morning, while many of the ferry companies offer a 'two for the price of one' deal on trips to the surrounding islands throughout this month. You'll also be able to get a discount on train tickets when you travel on Wednesdays.*

> **Boost your score!**
>
> In a multiple-choice task, you may hear all the options mentioned in the listening text. They will not necessarily be in the same order as they are given in the question. Don't rush and choose an option as soon as you hear it. Listen carefully to what is said and from what you hear, decide whether each option is correct or not.

2a Look at the following questions from Section 3 of the Listening test. <u>Underline</u> key words in each question. Question 1 has been done as an example. You have 30 seconds to read the questions before you listen.

---

1 What is <u>Hannah planning</u> to do <u>before</u> her next tutorial?
- **A** complete an essay
- **B** read up on relevant past events
- **C** speak to an expert in the field

2 What criticism do Hannah and Tom both make about a classmate's presentation?
- **A** the length of the talk was not appropriate
- **B** important details were missing
- **C** visual information was not clear

3 If Tom has any questions about a video project, Hannah recommends
- **A** speaking to their tutor.
- **B** asking other students.
- **C** looking at information online.

4 What does Tom think about current funding into research?
- **A** It illustrates a change in thinking.
- **B** It reflects present economic conditions.
- **C** It will have a significant effect on outcomes.

5 What surprised Hannah and Tom about the life and work of Dr Crow?
- **A** her educational background
- **B** her unusual career development
- **C** her legacy for future generations

2b 🎧 1 16 Listen and choose the correct answer, A, B or C.

3a 🎧 1 17 Look at the following question from Section 2 of a listening test. This is another type of multiple-choice task. Then listen and answer the question.

Choose **TWO** letters, **A–E**.

Which **TWO** facts are given about a trip to the forest?

- **A** People should bring food.

- **B** There will be a talk about nature.

- **C** The weather may be wet.

- **D** There will be a chance to swim.

- **E** Children can visit a play area.

3b 🎧 1 17 Listen again, and cross out the wrong options as you eliminate them. Were all the options mentioned?

📄 Look at the transcript on page 116 and check your answers.

Boost your score!

In this type of matching task, you can give your answers in any order, e.g. *1A, 2B* or *1B, 2A* - both are correct. While you are listening you should be able to eliminate some of the wrong answers, and it is a good idea to cross them out as you eliminate them.

✏ EXAM TASK

4 **Listen to a teacher giving a talk to new students.**

*Choose the correct letter, **A**, **B** or **C**.*

1   What event takes place on Wednesday?
   A   a language test
   B   a cultural celebration
   C   a meeting with past students

2   Which course ends in October?
   A   reading
   B   listening
   C   speaking

3   Students who wish to take exams should
   A   check their level with a teacher.
   B   enrol with the administrator.
   C   pay the exam fee now.

4   What are students advised to do if they are going to miss a class?
   A   tell a classmate
   B   phone the school
   C   arrange a meeting with their tutor

Questions 5 and 6

*Choose **TWO** letters, **A–E**.*

Which **TWO** things should students bring to their first lesson?

   A   a photograph

   B   a student card

   C   a dictionary

   D   a set of pens and pencils

   E   a completed form

5 **In pairs, check your answers with the transcript on pages 116 and 117. Underline the words that helped you choose the correct answers, then circle the distractors and give reasons why they were incorrect.**

Boost your score!

You can write on the question paper during the test, so underline key words in the question which will help you focus on what to listen out for. Underlining key words makes it easier to not be distracted by incorrect answers.

How to ... recognise paraphrases

1   Read the article once through. Work in pairs. Which building is shown in the photograph?

Indian palaces

Many of India's fabulously opulent royal homes are now open to the public as heritage hotels.

Few structures evoke the majesty of the Indian courts as splendidly as the country's numerous palaces and ancient forts. Each one offers a fascinating insight into India's immense historical and cultural diversity, from the haunting remains of the erstwhile Hindu Empire at Hampi to the many grand royal residences of the maharajas dotted throughout the state of Rajasthan.

At the time of independence in 1947 there were more than 550 princely states extending across the subcontinent. India's 'great kings' enjoyed extravagant lifestyles and, more often than not, expressed much of their wealth in spectacular buildings. Palaces were more than dwellings. These buildings served not just as royal residences but also as areas for public meetings called *durbars* and garrisons for troops.

Many palaces are now historic monuments, but to keep their homes financially viable, many owners have opened their properties to paying guests. Options vary from gargantuan palaces run by hotel chains to more modest residences, where you feel like you are staying with the family.

Rajasthan in India's north-west offers the largest concentration of the fairy-tale ideal of the grand residences and crumbling hilltop forts of the Rajputs and Mughals that ruled India for centuries.

As well as giving visitors the chance to observe at first-hand the luxurious lifestyle once enjoyed by the ruling elite, royal courts throughout Rajasthan also showcase the renowned talents of local craftspeople displayed in the ornate stonework, woodwork and decoration used throughout the buildings.

Known as the Pink City, owing to the rosy hue of its buildings, Jaipur was founded in 1727 by Maharaja Sawai Jai Singh, one of the greatest rulers of the Kachawaha clan of Rajput warriors. It is now firmly on the tourist trail, as one corner of the 'golden triangle' (Agra and Delhi are the other two). At the heart of Jaipur is the magnificent City Palace; it is still partly occupied by the royal family, who live in a wing called the Chandra Mahal.

Just outside the palace wall is one of Jaipur's most celebrated landmarks, the Hawa Mahal or 'Palace of the Winds', with a unique five-storey façade containing 953 windows intricately decorated. It was built in the late 18th century by Maharaja Pratap Singh to provide the ladies of his court with somewhere to watch the activity on the bustling streets below without being seen. The decoration also allows cool air into the building during the extremely hot summers.

Udaipur – one of Rajasthan's most romantic spots – is crowned by its sprawling city palace, built by ruler Udai

Singh in the 16th century as a strategic capital on the shores of Lake Pichola. While the lake is now fringed with many grand palaces and hotels, few can touch the Lake Palace. Floating in the middle of Lake Pichola, its cool white marble and mosaics make it one of Rajasthan's most instantly recognisable landmarks.

Further west, towards India's border with Pakistan, the fort in the remote desert city of Jaisalmer is another recommended stop. The fort's main square or *chowk* is dominated by the imposing Palace of the Maharawal. The stone façade was richly decorated by stonemasons of the Rajput ruler Rawal Jaisal in the 12th century and is deemed one of the best examples of its kind in India.

The splendid Umaid Bhawan Palace in Jodhpur takes some beating. One of the largest residences in the world, it was begun in 1928 by Maharaja Umaid Singh, grandfather of the present Maharaja of Jodhpur, who still lives with his family in a section of the palace. It is now one of India's most stunning heritage hotels.

2a   Find and <u>underline</u> the sentences in the article which each of the sentences below paraphrases.

a) Each palace provides an interesting insight into India's hugely diverse culture and history.

b) These buildings were for public and military use as well as being royal residences.

c) Many properties have been opened to paying guests.

d) Guests can see for themselves the wealthy way of life once enjoyed by the ruling elite.

e) Maharaja Sawai Jai Singh established Jaipur in 1727.

f) Maharaja Pratap Singh built the Hawa Mahal in the late 18th century and it allowed women from his court to watch the busy streets but remain unseen.

g) The intricately decorated twelfth-century façade is deemed one of the best examples of its kind in India.

h) There are not many heritage hotels as awe-inspiring as this one.

> **Boost your score!**
>
> Many different ways of paraphrasing will be used in the reading tasks. These ways are often used in combination.

2b   Work in pairs. Highlight and discuss the changes which have been made in the paraphrased sentences.

3   **Look back at the text and answer the questions.**

a)   How many different words for buildings can you find in the text? Look for specific words, e.g. *palace*, and general words, e.g. *structures*.

b)   Which noun is used as a verb to describe the City Palace's importance in Udaipur?

c)   The stonework of the Palace of the Maharawal is described as 'richly decorated'. What other words are used to describe carving in the text?

d)   All of these adjectives are used to describe buildings in this text. What differences are there in the meaning in these words?

> celebrated   crumbling   fascinating   gargantuan
> grand   instantly recognisable   modest
> opulent   stunning   unique

Boost your score!

Make a note of synonyms and paraphrases you find in reading passages to help increase your range of vocabulary. Explore the different shades of meaning in similar words and look out for words used in different forms too.

4   **Read the second part of the article before completing the exam tasks below.**

Agra is a must. While the Taj Mahal – Emperor Shah Jahan's most awe-inspiring legacy – might be India's most recognisable monument, there are other reasons to visit this one-time capital of the Mughals in Uttar Pradesh. Set on the banks of the Yamuna river, the sprawling UNESCO World Heritage-listed Agra Fort contains further significant examples of architecture from the Mughal period. The Mirror Palace, from whose tower there are inspiring views of the fort, is at its most magical around sunset.

Around 40 kilometres west of Agra, Fatehpur Sikri contains one of northern India's most impressive examples of a royal home, built by Emperor Akbar in the 16th century. It is now little more than a ghost city, yet it was the first planned city of the Mughal period, with a harmonious terraced layout.

One of the Indian capital's most striking landmarks is its Red Fort which was built as a residence for Shah Jahan in the 17th century when he moved the capital from Agra to Delhi. This fort, which occupies the northern edge of the atmospheric quarter of Old Delhi, contains several marble palaces, including the Rang Mahal or 'Painted Palace', which was home to the emperor's wives and mistresses. The fort also boasts India's largest mosque, the Jama Masjid.

The austere remains of Hampi, the last great Hindu kingdom of the Vijayanagara rulers, can be seen in the southern Indian state of Karnataka. Here fabulously wealthy princes built an impressive array of temples and palaces, mostly dating from the early 16th century. Subsequently abandoned, Hampi's boulder-strewn expanse is now one of southern India's most important heritage sites.

Further south, Mysore was home to one of the longest empires in Indian history, the Wodeyars, who established the city as their power base in the late 1400s. The present City Palace, designed by Henry Irwin in 1897, took the place of an earlier wooden structure that was destroyed by fire. Still home to the Maharaja of Mysore, the building has whimsical turrets, domes and colonnades. The palace is particularly spectacular when it is illuminated by more than 100,000 lights on Sundays, public holidays and during the ten days of the Hindu Dasara festival.

Taj Falaknuma Palace in Hyderabad in the state of Andhra Pradesh is an impressive Italian marble palace, the name of which translates as 'Mirror of the Sky'. The Taj Falaknuma Palace is a not very common blend of Italianate and Tudor architecture. Following a painstaking ten-year restoration of rooms laden with artefacts, frescoes, Venetian chandeliers and miles of parquet, it is one of India's most opulent new hotels.

Known as the City of Nizams, Hyderabad is worthy of plenty of exploration in its own right. It contains noteworthy landmarks such as the magnificent Charminar Palace in the centre of the old city, which was built in 1591 by Sultan Mohammad Quli Qutub Shah, and the Chowmahalla Palace, a cluster of four nineteenth-century palaces in Mughal and European styles which served as the official residence of the *nizam*, or 'administrator of the realm'.

The birthplace of Mahatma Gandhi, Gujarat is one of the subcontinent's lesser-visited states. However, it has fascinating historical sites as well as atmospheric palace hotels that feel more akin to a homestay. The UNESCO World Heritage-listed site Champaner-Pavagadh Archaeological Park, 50 kilometres from Baroda, is home to a number of sandstone monuments, mosques and palaces dating from the 8th to the 14th century and the largely unchanged Islamic pre-Mughal city of Champaner. It is an important pilgrimage destination for Hindus, who go to pray at its Kalika Mata Temple.

The small state of Chhattisgarh is home to the magnificent Kawardha Palace, a 140-kilometre drive from its capital city, Raipur. Set in the verdant greenery of the Maikal mountain range, this palace, built in the 1930s, is a fascinating architectural fusion of British, Mughal and Italian architecture.

✏️ EXAM TASK

5

*Complete each sentence with the correct ending, **A–H,** below.*

1 The Taj Mahal is not the only building in Agra showcasing

2 Shah Jahan built his impressive fort after changing

3 The City Palace in Mysore was constructed as

4 Taj Falaknuma Palace is a hotel that required

5 Between the 8th and 14th centuries builders in the Baroda region created

6 The Kawardha Palace was built in the 1930s and incorporates

A 3	a replacement for another building on the same site.
B 2	the location of a principal city.
C 5	structures from a particular material.
D 4	a site for annual festivities.
E 1	important architectural features from the Mughal Empire.
F 4	careful renovation which took place over a number of years.
G	spectacular views from the region.
H 6	architectural ideas from more than one country.

✏️ EXAM TASK

6

Look at the following statements (Questions 7–13) and the list of cities below.

*Match each statement with the correct city, **A–D**.*

NB You may use any letter more than once.

7 The location of a landmark which is lit up one day a week. D

8 A place that is often referred to by another name.

9 The home of a monument that is very well-known. A

10 A city near a site which is often visited by worshippers.

11 The whereabouts of a palace which has an unusual mixture of architectural styles.

12 The setting for a waterside fort.

13 A settlement which does not differ much from its original appearance.

A	Agra	**C**	Hyderabad
B	Champaner	**D**	Mysore

7 **What paraphrases and synonyms did you notice in the exam tasks in exercises 5 and 6?**

90 mins

How to ... develop complex sentences

1a **Look at the Writing Task 2 question.**

Some people think that a prison sentence is a punishment for bad behaviour. Other people claim that prisoners should be given help to change their behaviour.

What is your view?

Read the two extracts from essays answering the question. Which has more complex sentences, A or B?

A

Some people believe that the main purpose of prison is to be a punishment for criminals. Others believe that punishment is not the only purpose of prison. They think prison should help criminals to change their behaviour. I think prison should do both things. Criminals need rehabilitation. This means advising them how to become a good member of society again.

Prisons often do not educate prisoners because of the cost. Keeping people locked in cells is cheaper than teaching them to change. Some members of our society believe that people who commit a crime deserve to be punished. The possibility of a strict punishment should stop people from wanting to commit crimes.

B

Some people believe that the main purpose of prison is to be a punishment for criminals, while others believe that punishment is not the only purpose of prison. They think prison should help criminals to change their behaviour. In my own view, prison should do both things. Criminals need rehabilitation, which means advising them how to become a good member of society again.

One of the main reasons that prisons often do not educate prisoners is the cost. Keeping people locked in cells is cheaper than teaching them to change. Furthermore, some members of our society believe that if someone has committed a crime, they deserve to be punished. In addition, the possibility of a strict punishment should stop people from wanting to commit crimes.

1b **What type of language does the writer use to make longer sentences in Essay B?**

2a **Look at the following sentences. The relative pronoun in each sentence is <u>underlined</u>. What does it refer to in each case?**

a) It is difficult to argue with doctors <u>who</u> have many years of experience of working in hospitals.

b) Immunisation, <u>which</u> is giving people injections to prevent disease, is used in most developed countries.

c) Celebrities have to accept that they may be followed by photographers and journalists, <u>who</u> make money selling pictures to the newspapers.

d) There are several large parks in the capital city in my country <u>where</u> people go to relax and enjoy nature.

e) In general elections, people have the opportunity to vote for politicians <u>whose</u> policies and decisions will affect everyone's lives.

f) It is sometimes said that improving air pollution is the duty of government, <u>which</u> allows individuals to avoid responsibility.

> **Boost your score!**
>
> In Task 2 you have the chance to write approximately 250 words in an essay, and to achieve a band 7, you need to use a variety of complex sentences. Although you can and should still use short sentences with one clause (e.g. *Some people think taxes are too high*); you also need to show that you can use sentences with more than one clause (e.g. *Some people think that, due to recent increases, taxes are too high.*).

2b **Match the clauses in 1–6 with a–f.**

1 Whenever the temperature drops,

2 As soon as the law is changed,

3 The number of cars would fall

4 If people had acted sooner,

5 People continue to fly regularly,

6 As well as making recycling easier,

a pollution will decrease.

b if road tax was higher.

c we need to raise awareness about its importance.

d demand for electricity goes up.

e even though it is bad for the planet.

f climate change might have been prevented.

3 **Use the notes below to write a paragraph containing at least two complex sentences, using structures from the activities in this lesson.**

> *Some people believe that the most effective way of reducing pollution is to increase taxes on petrol.*
>
> *Do you agree or disagree?*
>
> *(Disagree)* - *Main cause of pollution is factories & big business*
>
> - *Not fair to punish individuals*
>
> - *Higher petrol tax = expensive to drive a car and travel by plane (only affects individuals)*

Boost your score!

Use a variety of styles for writing complex sentences.

✎ EXAM TASK

4 **Look at the following Task 2 question. Include a range of short and complex sentences in your answer.**

You should spend about 40 minutes on this task.

Write about the following topic:

> *Some people think that due to the popularity of technology and the internet for reading and researching online, public libraries will soon become unnecessary and no longer exist.*
>
> *What is your view?*

Give reasons for your answer and include any relevant examples from your own knowledge or experience.

Write at least 250 words.

5 **Compare your answer with the sample answer. Which examples of complex structures from the lesson can you identify? Did you use similar structures or different ones?**

How to ... structure the long turn

1a   **Look at the following Part 2 question.**

> Describe a present you gave to someone.
>
> You should say
>
>> who the present was for
>>
>> what the present was
>>
>> why you chose the present
>
> and say whether the present was a good choice.

Boost your score!

You do not have to talk about all the bullet points, but they can give you ideas of what to talk about. Talking about each bullet point in turn can help to structure your talk.

1b   🎧 **1 19** **Listen to someone answering the following question in two different ways. As you listen to each talk, put a tick under each topic as the speaker mentions it.**

	Who the present was for	What the present was	Why you chose the present	Whether the present was a good choice
Talk 1				
Talk 2				

1c   **Which talk is most clearly organised? Why?**

1d   **Now do the task yourself in pairs. You have one minute to make notes. Try to organise ideas logically when planning. Change roles and repeat.**

2a   🎧 **1 20** **Read and listen to a student talking about a hobby they enjoy doing. What function do the underlined words have?**

'The hobby I enjoy most is painting, <u>which</u> is something I have been doing since I was a child. I started painting at school in art lessons <u>and</u> I enjoyed it very much. I had a good art teacher <u>who</u> helped me and she made me want to be an artist, <u>but</u> I wasn't good enough for that! <u>Anyway</u>, these days I still paint as a hobby, <u>in fact</u> I did some painting a few days ago. I find it very relaxing so I often paint when I feel stressed, <u>for example</u>, when I have a lot of work to do or I am preparing for exams. <u>As for</u> how often I paint, well, probably about once or twice a month <u>because</u> I am busy with my studies these days.'

2b   **The underlined words above are sometimes described as linking devices. Put each one into the right category according to use. An example has been done for you.**

Giving additional information   ....

Describing cause and result   ....

Giving contrasting information   ....

Relative pronouns   *which* ....

Changing topic   ....

2c **Look at the following extracts. Add linking devices from above and from your own knowledge to improve the coherence of the texts.**

a)

'My favourite day of the week is Saturday. I like ~~Saturday. On~~ Saturday I *it because on* don't work and I usually go to the park. At the park I enjoy walking and taking photos of the beautiful landscape. Sometimes I visit the café. I buy a drink. Sometimes I meet my friends in the café. I chat with my friends. In the evenings I often go out. I go to the cinema or to a restaurant.'

b)

'An important moment in my life was when I got a new job. I got the new job last year. The new job was a shop assistant in a bookshop. I have always wanted to work in a bookshop. I love books and reading. Before the new job, I worked in a newsagent's. I didn't like working in the newsagent's. It was boring.'

> **Boost your score!**
>
> To achieve a band 7 or higher, you need to use a range of discourse markers or linking devices with flexibility. It is not necessary to use the most formal linking devices that you might use for writing, but using simple, informal linking devices will improve the coherence of your talk.

2d 🎧 **1 21** **Listen to the following extract. Does this speaker use linking devices effectively? Why / Why not?**

✎ EXAM TASK

3a **Work in pairs. Student A – look at Task A. Student B – look at Task B. Spend 1 minute thinking about what you are going to say and making notes.**

Task A

Describe a toy you used to like playing with as a child.

You should say

      what the toy was

      where you got the toy from

      why you liked playing with it

and say whether you learned anything from playing with the toy.

Task B

Describe a job you would like to do in the future.

You should say

      what the job is

      when you would like to do the job

      why you would like to do the job

and say whether you think it is likely that you will do this job one day.

3b **In your pairs, take turns to talk about the topic. You should talk about the topic for one to two minutes.**

LISTENING

 **SECTION 1**

Questions 1–10

Complete the notes below.

*Write **ONE WORD AND/OR A NUMBER** for each answer.*

Running club application

> *Example*
>
> Name: Grace (**0**) ....*Taylor*.........

Personal Details

Year of birth: **1** ....

Address: 63 **2** ....*West Horton*.... Road

Phone number: **3** .... ○┄┄┄┄┄┄┄

Email: gtaylor@talkmail.com

Profession: **4** ....

💡 How do we say phone numbers in English?

Health and Fitness

Group interested in **5** ....

Other sports: **6** ....

Health issues: pain in **7** ....

Other information

Will need a T-shirt in **8** .... size ○┄┄┄┄┄┄┄┄┄

Heard about the club from **9** ....

Has a son who might want to join – aged **10** ....

💡 What are the possible options for this answer?

 SECTION 2

Questions 11–13

Which group of volunteers will be given the following duties?

*Choose **THREE** answers from the box and write the correct letter, **A–D**, next to the Questions 11–13.*

Talk for volunteers at a Country House

11 Group 1 ....

12 Group 2 ....

13 Group 3 ....

Duties
A serving food in the café
B answering emails in the office
C taking payment in the shop
D showing guests around the gardens

What vocabulary do you associate with the duties?

e.g. **C** customers / purchase / buy

How could you paraphrase the terms in the box?

e.g. **A** food – snacks
     C payment – money

Questions 14–20

Complete the notes below.

Write **NO MORE THAN TWO WORDS AND / OR A NUMBER** for each answer.

Events	Details
History Tours	Training will be given Maximum group size **14** ....
15 .... visits	At least one a week
Musical performances	**Look after** the **16** ....
Art exhibits	Hand out **17** .... Take orders from buyers
Workshops	Help prepare materials Includes painting and **18** ....
Special events (e.g. **19** ....)	Need extra help in the **20** ....

You'll hear more than one number, so listen carefully.

What is another way of saying 'look after'?

 **SECTION 3**

Questions 21–25

*Choose the correct letter, **A**, **B** or **C**.*

Western Medicine in the 19th Century

21 How do the students describe medicine **in the early 1800s**?
    A   undergoing rapid change
    B   extremely basic
    C   surprisingly sophisticated

> Read the question carefully and pay close attention to the time period they are discussing – the answer here must be about 'the early 1800s'.

22 What was the main strength of Maggie's presentation?
    A   the originality of the visuals
    B   the range of examples
    C   the organisation of ideas

23 What change to hospitals at the end of the 1800s were the students surprised to read about?
    A   the sudden increase in the number of hospital beds
    B   the injection of funding to build newer hospitals
    C   the development of specialist hospitals

24 Dan and Maggie **both** agree that by the 1900s
    A   the advances in medicine were not as great as sometimes claimed.
    B   techniques used in surgery had undergone enormous change.
    C   doctors finally had their profession respected.

> The students could have different opinions about the points in options **A**, **B** and **C**, but they must **both** agree about the correct answer.

25 Which cause of medical progress does Dan decide to focus on in his essay?
    A   the Industrial Revolution
    B   scientific knowledge
    C   social factors

Questions 26–30

What criticism do the speakers make about using books by the following authors?

*Choose **FIVE** answers from the box and write the correct letter, **A–G**, next to Questions 26–30.*

Criticisms

A	it's not wholly relevant to their topic
B	it contains generalisations
C	it is difficult to follow some of its arguments
D	it is out of date
E	it is not detailed enough
F	its conclusions are not supported by evidence
G	it is not very original

---

26 James Pinkerton ....

27 Maria Saville ....

28 Bruce Daniels ....

29 Ellen Minton ....

30 Deborah Dey ....

THINK IT THROUGH

There are seven options for five questions, so two of the options **A–G** are just distractors. Listen carefully – a similar sounding word is not necessarily the right answer. For example, the recording mentions that the book 'gives a good general overview', but is this the same as a 'generalisation' (item **B**)?

 SECTION 4

Questions 31–33

Choose the correct letter A, B or C.

A Study of Koalas

31   What was the original motivation for the study?
   A   concern about effects of climate change
   B   alarm about the declining koala population
   C   interest in tree conservation

32   What were scientists **surprised** to learn?
   A   that koalas depend on trees for food and shelter
   B   that koalas are reliant on different species of trees
   C   that koalas could survive without eucalyptus trees

> These options may all be true, but which was 'surprising'?

33   The most significant discovery was made with data gathered by
   A   cameras.
   B   weather stations.
   C   tracking collars.

Questions 34–40

Complete the notes below.

*Write **ONE WORD ONLY** for each answer.*

The **34** .... of koalas in a tree is vital in optimising the cooling power of trees.

The fur is thinnest on a **koala's 35** ...., which affects its behaviour.

> Notice the possessive 's' before the gap – what does this tell you about the answer?

Koalas stay near the top of trees during **36** ....

Acacia trees use more **37** .... than other trees.

The plant is cooled in a similar way to the use of **38** .... in humans.

Koalas are at risk from

• **developments** such as agriculture, industry and **39** ....

• attacks from pets

• being hit by **40** .... at night

> What other modern developments could affect the natural world?

READING

Make a photocopy of the Reading test answer sheet on page 109.

READING PASSAGE 1

*You should spend about 20 minutes on **Questions 1–13**, which are based on Reading Passage 1 below.*

Out of Africa

Stone tools rewrite history of man as a global species

A stone-age archaeological site in the Arabian peninsula has become the focus of a radical theory of how early humans made the long walk from their evolutionary homeland of Africa to become a globally-dispersed species. Scientists have found a set of stone tools buried beneath a collapsed rock shelter in the barren hills of the United Arab Emirates that they believe were made about 125,000 years ago by people who had migrated out of eastern Africa by crossing the Red Sea when sea levels were at a record low.

The age of the stone tools and the fact they appear to be like those made by anatomically-modern humans living in eastern Africa suggests that our species, Homo sapiens, left Africa between 30,000 and 55,000 years earlier than previously believed. This casts new light on how modern humans eventually inhabited lands as far apart as Europe and Australia. Genetic evidence had suggested that modern humans made the main migration from Africa between 60,000 and 70,000 years ago, although there was always a possibility of earlier migrations that had not got much further than the Middle East. However, all these movements were believed to have been made into the Middle East by people walking down the Nile valley.

However, the stone tools unearthed at the Jebel Faya site about 50 kilometres from the Persian Gulf suggests another possible migratory route across the Bab al-Mandab strait, a tract of open water which separates the Red Sea from the Arabian Ocean and the Horn of Africa from the Arabian Peninsula. The scientists behind the study said that at the time of the migration, about 125,000 years ago, sea levels would have been low enough for people to make the crossing on foot or with simple rafts or watercraft. They also suggest that the waterless Nejd plateau of southern Arabia, which would have posed another barrier to migration, was in fact at that time covered in lakes.

'By 130,000 years ago, the sea level was still about 100 metres lower than at present while the Nejd plateau was already passable. There was a brief period where modern humans may have been able to use the direct route from East Africa to Jebel Faya,' said Professor Adrian Parker of Oxford Brookes University, who was part of the research team. Once humans had crossed into southern Arabia, they would have enjoyed the benefits of a land rich in wildlife and, with little competition, the migrant community could have quickly expanded to become an important secondary centre for population growth, which later migrated across the Persian Gulf to India, and from there to the rest of Asia, the scientists suggest.

Simon Armitage of Royal Holloway, University of London, the lead author of the study published in the journal Science, said that discovering the dates of the stone tools was the key piece of evidence suggesting there was a much earlier migration out of Africa than previously supposed. 'Archaeology without ages is like a jigsaw with the interlocking edges removed – you have lots of individual pieces of information but you can't fit them together to produce the big picture,' Dr Armitage said. 'At Jebel Faya, the ages reveal a fascinating picture in which modern humans migrated out of Africa much earlier than previously thought, helped by global fluctuations in sea level and the climate change in the Arabian Peninsula.'

The stone 'tool kit' found at Jebel Faya includes relatively primitive hand axes and a collection of stone scrapers and perforators. The scientists say the tools resemble artefacts found in eastern Africa and their primitive nature suggests that migration did not depend on the invention of more complex tools. 'These anatomically modern humans, like you and me, had evolved in Africa about 200,000 years ago and subsequently populated the rest of the world. Our findings should stimulate a re-evaluation of the means by which we modern humans became a global species,' Dr Armitage said.

However, not all scientist are convinced. Paul Mellars of Cambridge University told Science: 'I'm totally unpersuaded. There's not a scrap of evidence here that these were made by modern humans, nor that they came from Africa.'

Questions 1–6

Do the following statements agree with the information given in Reading Passage 1?

In boxes 1–6 on your answer sheet, write

TRUE	*if the statement agrees with the information*
FALSE	*if the statement contradicts the information*
NOT GIVEN	*if there is no information on this*

1   According to Dr Armitage, determining the age of the 'tool kit' proves that there was earlier migration from Africa.

2   Dr Armitage rejects traditional archaeological research methods.

3   Changes in geography and weather patterns assisted migration out of Africa.

4   The 'tool kit' found at Jebel Faya was unusually large.

5   Dr Armitage said that migration relied on the invention of sophisticated tools.

6   Paul Mellars believes the 'tool kit' originated in Africa.

 THINK IT THROUGH

Identify exactly what is being tested in a question before reading for the answer.

In Question 2, the focus is research **methods**. Dr Armitage rejects the opinions of other researchers (the research **findings**) but there is no mention of him criticising how they did their research (the research **methods**).

Choose **Not Given** when there is no information given about this statement in the text.

Questions 7–13

Complete the notes below.

Choose **NO MORE THAN TWO WORDS AND/OR A NUMBER** from the passage for each answer.

Write your answers in boxes 7–13 on your answer sheet.

Stone tools rewrite history

The tools were:

- located in the United Arab Emirates under a fallen **7** ....
- about 125 000 years old
- made by migrants travelling overland due to low water levels
- produced by people from **8** ....

This research challenges previous theories by:

- suggesting early humans migrated earlier than previously believed
- disputing previous claims that humans left Africa no more than **9** .... years ago
- questioning whether all people travelled along the **10** .... to their final destination

These new theories propose that:

- an alternative migratory route was used across the Bab al-Mandab strait
- people could cross by boat or **11** ....
- southern Arabia offered migrants opportunities to hunt for **12** ....
- migrants then moved on into India and some to other places in **13** ....

READING PASSAGE 2

*You should spend about 20 minutes on **Questions 14–27**, which are based on Reading Passage 2 below.*

Questions 14–19

Reading Passage 2 has six paragraphs, **A–F**.

Choose the correct heading for each paragraph from the list of headings below.

*Write the correct number, **i–viii**, in boxes 14–19 on your answer sheet.*

List of Headings
i   Understanding people who react strongly to smell
ii   Future awards for research expected
iii   Everyone has a different capacity for smell
iv   The variety of reactions to smell
v   The development of our sense of smell
vi   Applications of smell research
vii   Disagreement over research findings
viii   Research into smell eventually received award

14   Paragraph **A**

15   Paragraph **B**

16   Paragraph **C**

17   Paragraph **D**

18   Paragraph **E**

19   Paragraph **F**

THINK IT THROUGH

Matching headings

Choose the heading that best summarises the **whole** paragraph. Some options might be mentioned in several paragraphs, but they are not the main idea.

For example, paragraphs B and E both talk about an individual's capacity for smell (option iii) but the focus of paragraph E is people who react strongly to smell (option i).

The smelling test:
The genetics of olfaction

A Why are some people more sensitive to odours than others? And why do no two people experience a scent in the same way? The answer lies in our genes. In 2004 neuroscientists Linda Buck and Richard Axel shared a Nobel Prize for their identification of the genes that control smell, findings which they first published in the early 1990s. Their work revived interest in the mysterious workings of our noses – interest which is now generating some surprising insights, not least that each of us inhabits our own personal olfactory world.

B 'When I give talks, I always say that everybody in this room smells the world with a different set of receptors, and therefore it smells different to everybody,' says Andreas Keller, a geneticist working at the Rockefeller University in New York City. He also suspects that every individual has at least one odorant he or she cannot detect at all – one specific anosmia, or olfactory 'blind spot', which is inherited along with his or her olfactory apparatus. The human nose contains roughly 400 olfactory receptors, each of which responds to several odorants, and each of which is encoded by a different gene. But, unless you are dealing with identical twins, no two persons will have the same genetic make-up for those receptors.

C The reason, according to Doron Lancet, a geneticist at the Weizmann Institute of Science in Israel, is that those genes have been accumulating mutations over evolution. This has happened in all the great apes, and one possible explanation is that smell has gradually become less important to survival, having been replaced to some extent by colour vision – as an indicator of rotten fruit, for example, or of a potentially venomous predator. However, every species has a different genetic 'bar code' and a different combination of olfactory sensitivities.

D That genetic variability is reflected in behavioural variability, as Keller recently demonstrated when they asked 500 people to rate 66 odours for intensity and pleasantness. The responses covered the full range from intense to weak, and from pleasant to unpleasant, with most falling in the moderate range – a classic bell curve in each case. The researchers also tested people's subconscious responses to odorants, by presenting them at much weaker doses. One compound that people famously perceive differently is androstenone, a substance that is produced in boars' testes and is also present in some people's sweat. 'For about 50 per cent of people androstenone is nothing,' says Chuck Wysocki of the Monell Chemical Senses Center in Philadelphia. 'For 35 per cent it's a very powerful stale urine smell, and for 15 per cent it's a floral, musky, woody note.'

E Lancet says that the genetic tools that are now available could help researchers to solve another olfactory puzzle, too: why some people have an acute overall sensitivity to smells than others. One in 5,000 people is born without any sense of smell at all, while at the other end of the spectrum are those individuals who have a higher than average general sensitivity, some of whom may gravitate to the perfume industry. He suspects that the biological culprits in this case are not the olfactory receptors themselves, which are responsible for specific anosmias, but the proteins that ensure the efficient transmission of the signals elicited by those receptors to higher processing areas in the brain – transmission pathways that are shared by all receptors. 'What is fascinating to me is the idea that we could discover a gene or genes that underlie this general sensitivity to odorants, so that we might be able to 'type' those professional noses and say, 'A-ha, we now understand why you are in your profession,' Lancet says.

F The implications of the new research go wider than smell, however. Most of our sensation of taste comes from the odorants in food stimulating our olfactory receptors. 'The wonderful enjoyment of a fresh tomato is practically only in the nose,' Lancet says. Awareness of individual variation in smell has already filtered through to the wine world, launching a debate about how valuable experts' advice really is, when they may be having different smell – and hence taste – experiences from other people. The science of smell could even throw light on patterns of human disease. Thanks to Buck and Axel, scientists now know a lot more about the genetics of olfaction, which the Nobel Prize committee may or may not have foreseen when they bestowed their honour in 2004.

Boost your score!

Reading is a great way to improve your English and increase the range of your vocabulary. Try to read something in English every day.

- Choose carefully. If you are choosing something to read for pleasure, aim for a text which has no more than ten new words per page. Graded readers are a good option. Check out our range of higher-level readers at www.scholasticieltreaders.co.uk.

- Reading non-fiction texts is an excellent way to learn new topic words. Choose something to read which you know you will enjoy, such as a magazine or newspaper article or a web page about something you are interested in or need to find out. Many non-fiction texts include photos which will help with understanding.

Questions 20–23

Look at the following statements (Questions 20–23) and the list of people below.

Match each statement with the correct person, **A–D**.

Write the correct letter, **A–D**, in boxes 20–23 on your answer sheet.

NB   You may use any letter more than once.

20   No individual has a perfect sense of smell.

21   Around one third of individuals disagree on a particular smell.

22   **Studies show** that the majority of people react to smell in similar ways.

23   The sense of smell has lost priority to sight.

Item 22 paraphrases an idea in the text. Look for information in the text which is related to 'studies', e.g. *experiments, research, results*.

List of People

A   Axel and Buck

B   Keller

C   Lancet

D   Wysocki

Questions 24–27

Complete the summary below.

Choose **ONE WORD ONLY** from the passage for each answer.

Write your answers in boxes 24–27 on your answer sheet.

The olfactory puzzle: who is super-sensitive to smells?

Lancet believes researchers have the genetic tools to find the answer to why certain people display

24 .... reactions to smells in general. While some people may have no sense of smell, others

are highly sensitive and in some cases, may end up working in the **25** .... business. Lancet

believes the biological reason behind a heightened sense of smell is **26** .... in the body which

help signals transmit to the brain. He hopes that scientists can identify a **27** .... which would

identify those who are particularly sensitive to smell.

READING PASSAGE 3

You should spend about 20 minutes on **Questions 28–40***, which are based on Reading Passage 3 below.*

Georgia O'Keeffe's Exhibition at the Tate Modern

An extraordinary show, long overdue

The major retrospective of Georgia O'Keeffe's work that opened this week at the Tate Modern art gallery in London, UK, is a rare opportunity for British viewers to engage with this revered American artist. In the same season as the opening of the Tate extension Switch House, this exhibition illuminates the gallery's determination to provide new readings of old favourites. Curator Tanya Barson has spun a new tale of O'Keeffe, showing her as a progressive artist who was influenced by photography and not 'merely an observational painter'. The inclusion of photography, while interesting, again shows a lack of confidence by the institution to let a singular medium prevail.

Georgia O'Keeffe was born in Wisconsin in 1887 and died in 1986 aged 98. She married the great photographer Alfred Steiglitz in 1924, who promoted O'Keeffe in both his own gallery as well as with his extensive circle of friends. Ironically, it was he who put forward the idea that the flowers she famously painted were indeed erotic interpretations, a reading that O'Keeffe strenuously denied through her long life.

I start with this context so we don't forget the long history of over-looked women artists, not that O'Keeffe was one of these. The Museum of Modern Art in New York held a retrospective of her work in 1946. Her red poppies appeared on a US postage stamp, and her home in the US state of New Mexico, now open to the public, still attracts a pilgrimage of worshipping tourists, both female and male. Her best-known subject matter is the large and eye-catching flowers.

In this exhibition the paintings are arranged roughly chronologically and embrace her time spent in New York City following her marriage to Steiglitz, as well as in Lake George, where she spent every summer during this period. Her New York paintings, often created from a high perspective, encapsulate a city of skyscrapers bathed in a dramatic night-time light. While her time spent in Lake George reflects her engagement with a verdant landscape, here she wrote 'I feel smothered with green'.

O'Keeffe was fiercely independent and continued to be so well into her later years. She was a hiker, going 'tramping' in all weathers, visiting and revisiting sites often remote from her home. This pioneering spirit led to her preoccupations with objects and views that she personally experienced.

While O'Keeffe's paintings of closely observed blossoms are loved by many, the room of these is sadly not the most powerful room here, perhaps due to loan restrictions. Some of the great floral blooms, including the luxurious purple iris, are not here, but there is *Jimson Weed* (1932), a painting that became well-known in 2014 when it became, at $44.4m (£34.2m), the most expensive by a female artist ever sold at auction. Nearby are beautifully observed still lifes, an eggplant, figs and an alligator pear in all their majestic simplicity. We are told that these are a result of O'Keeffe looking at photography. Yet this is an artist who constantly reacted to locations with her own eyes.

O'Keeffe discovered Ghost Ranch in New Mexico – the property that was to become her home – in 1934, finally purchasing the house in 1940. The view from the ranch of a flat-topped tableland, became her favoured view. She painted and repainted it, saying at one point: 'God told me if I painted it enough I could have it.' She also discovered the 'Black Place', another location she revisited throughout her life whilst driving through the Navajo country. These abstract black hills recurred throughout her work and became one of the locations of seriality. Over time she worked through different permutations while also moving towards abstraction, the strong natural forms reduced into powerful symbols.

O'Keeffe was perhaps the first artist to paint views seen from an airplane; her aerial shots of fluffy clouds and the horizontality of the sky produced from memories of her flights from New York City to New Mexico. Again this is credited to her husband's photographs of the sky and clouds, but when you stand in front of her *Sky Above the Clouds III* you can see the painterly licence that O'Keeffe adopted, making this painting much more memorable than the Steiglitz photographs, lovely though they are.

This is an extraordinary show, a collection of nearly 100 works celebrating a woman artist, long overdue in this country. I think that a quote from her sums up this rewarding if flawed exhibition: 'A woman who has lived many things and who sees lines and colours as an expression of living might say something that a man can't – I feel there is something unexplored about women that only a woman can explore – the men have done all they can do about it.'

Questions 28–32

*Complete each sentence with the correct ending, **A–H**, below.*

28   The writer believes that this exhibition gives the public

29   The Tate Modern hopes its exhibitions will offer

30   Tanya Barson says this exhibition presents

31   The writer states that exhibiting photography alongside the paintings is

32   Alfred Steiglitz insisted that the flowers in his wife's art represented

A	evidence of the impact that photography had on O'Keeffe.
B	a comment on O'Keeffe's relationship with her husband.
C	a good chance to see O'Keeffe's work.
D	nature in a sensual manner.
E	proof that multi-media exhibitions are important.
F	a reinterpretation of popular artwork.
G	an example of the gallery not taking risks.
H	the finest collection of O'Keeffe's work ever shown.

THINK IT THROUGH

This question type (matching sentence endings) can be tricky because there may be several endings that seem plausible. Locate the information in the text and read it again very carefully to determine which sentence ending is **completely** true.

For example, question 30 could end with **A**, **C**, **F**, **G** or **H**. However, the question is about Tanya Barson's views, so to answer this question you need to locate Barson's name in the text and find her opinion on the exhibition.

Questions 33 and 34

*Choose **TWO** letters, **A–E**.*

In the second paragraph, the writer makes some statements about O'Keeffe's career.

Which of these **TWO** statements are mentioned by the writer of the text?

A   Her work does not receive the attention it deserves because she is female.

B   The 1946 exhibition failed to attract large numbers of people.

C   O'Keeffe remains popular with fans today.

D   O'Keeffe's work is mainly popular amongst women.

E   Her depiction of flowers in her paintings is why she is well-known.

THINK IT THROUGH

The references to items **C**, **D** and **E** all come from the same paragraph in the passage. Which paragraph is it?

Questions 35 and 36

*Choose **TWO** letters, **A–E**.*

The list below gives some possible opinions about *Jimson Weed*.

Which **TWO** of the following statements are made by the writer of the text?

A   It makes the other paintings exhibited look simple in comparison.

B   It is a fine example of O'Keeffe's flower paintings.

C   It is not a forceful example of O'Keeffe's work.

D   It is famous because of its value.

E   It was borrowed from another institution at an excessively high cost.

The information about the painting *Jimson Weed* is in one paragraph of the passage only. Find this paragraph and read it in detail.

Questions 37–40

Complete the table below.

Choose **ONE WORD AND/OR A NUMBER** *from the passage for each answer.*

O'Keeffe's Work in Different Locations

THINK IT THROUGH

Use the list of places to help you navigate to the section of the passage where the information is given. Then read this section of the passage in detail to find the answer.

PLACE	TIME	THE IMPACT OF LOCATION ON HER ART
New York	• moved here after getting married	• viewed scenes from above • painted the city in the evening using **37** .... colours
Lake George	• stayed here in the **38** .... months	• surrounded by lush vegetation
New Mexico, *Ghost Ranch*	• bought property as her home in **39**	• repainted the landscape nearby many times
Navajo country, *Black Place*	• drove through the area on many occasions	• repeatedly painted the hills until they became **40** .... which hardly resembled the landscape

WRITING

TASK 1

You should spend about 20 minutes on this task.

> *The pie charts below give information about the satisfaction levels of customers of a café in January and then in August in the same year.*
>
> *Summarise the information by selecting and reporting the main features, and make comparisons where relevant.*

Write at least 150 words.

THINK IT THROUGH

Identify the most significant changes. Which area shows the biggest increase or decrease over the time period? Which area are customers most and least satisfied with?

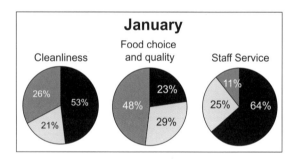

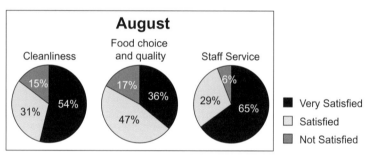

TASK 2

You should spend about 40 minutes on this task.

Write about the following topic:

> *In the past, most employed people went to a place of work to do their jobs. These days, more and more people are choosing to work from home.*
>
> *What are the reasons for this change?*
>
> *Is this a positive or a negative development?*

Give reasons for your answer and include any relevant examples from your own knowledge or experience.

Write at least 250 words.

THINK IT THROUGH

Include **reasons** for the change in working practices as well as discussion about whether this is a **positive** or **negative** change.

SPEAKING

PART 1: Introduction and interview

Dancing

- Do you like dancing? Why? / Why not?

- How important is dancing in your country? Why? / Why not?

- Do you enjoy watching dance performances? Why? / Why not?

- Is there any style of dancing that you would like to learn how to do? Why? / Why not?

> Don't panic if you don't like dancing! You can still talk about **why not**.

PART 2: Individual long turn

You will have to talk about the topic for one to two minutes.

You have one minute to think about what you are going to say.

You can make some notes to help you if you wish.

> Describe a time when you learned to do something **difficult**.
>
> You should say
>
>   what you learned to do
>
>   why you decided to learn to do it
>
>   how you learned to do it
>
> and say whether it has been useful to you.

> Remember to refer to what you found **difficult** in your answer. Read the topic card carefully and ensure that you answer the question accurately.

Final question

Do you enjoy learning new things?

PART 3: Two-way discussion

Learning difficult things

What can people do to stay motivated when trying to learn difficult things?

Has the development of technology made learning easier? Why? / Why not?

How important is it to have support from other people when trying to learn difficult things? Why? / Why not?

Success and failure

What are some of the different definitions people have of success (e.g. money, a good job etc.)? Why?

Is it necessary to experience failure to become successful? Why? / Why not?

> **Boost your score!**
>
> 🎧 2 5 – 🎧 2 7 Listen to Takeshi's Speaking test. Which of his answers do you think are particularly good? In pairs, discuss why.

45 mins

How to ... prepare for listening tasks

1a 🎧 **2 8** **Look at the following questions, with answers given by candidates. All the answers given are incorrect. Listen to the recording, and correct the answers.**

Write **ONE WORD AND/OR A NUMBER** for each answer.

a) There is a picture of a _____*big tree*_____ on the wall.

b) The manager's name is John _____*Clark*_____ .

c) Each presentation should last no longer than _____*10 minutes*_____ .

d) There will be a _____*brake*_____ at lunchtime.

e) The decision will be announced in _____*Thursday*_____ .

> **Boost your score!**
>
> Pay close attention to the number of words you need to write - if the question says **NO MORE THAN TWO WORDS** and you write three words, the answer will be incorrect.

1b **What type of mistake has been made in each case?**

1c **Work with a partner. What general tip could you give to the candidate to help with each type of mistake?**

Example: Question b – listen carefully to the correct spelling and write the exact letters that you hear

2 **Look at the map of an island. Work in pairs to write a short description of the location of A–F. Use the words in the box to help you if necessary.**

Example: A is on the north-west coast.

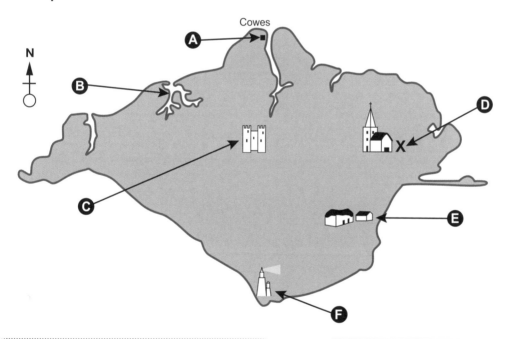

> north / south / east / west (of)
> in the north east / south west
> on the north east coast / on the south west coast
> next to / near / below / above / alongside (the)
> at the top / bottom (of the map)
> on the left / right-hand side (of the map)
> in the centre / in the middle (of)

> **Boost your score!**
>
> Before the test, make sure you know the vocabulary used to describe where things are located. This is a relatively small set of vocabulary, so make yourself familiar with commonly used expressions. If you have a map labelling task in the test, use the preparation time to think about this vocabulary and how it might be used. Notice any clues on the diagram, such as a compass symbol.

3a Look at the diagram of a wind turbine below. Work in pairs and discuss how you could describe where each label is placed on the diagram.

Example: A – *next to the blade / between the blade and the gearbox*

3b 🎧 Now, listen to an engineer describing how the turbine works. Match the parts 1–5 with the labels on the diagram A–E.

Parts of a wind turbine

1   transformer   **3**   motor   **5**   device to measure wind

2   generator   **4**   brake

3c 📄 Look at the transcript on page 122. Did the speaker use any of the same expressions you had predicted?

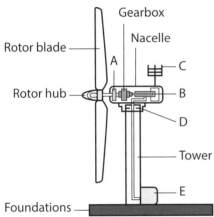

> ### Boost your score!
>
> Look at where the labels are so you are ready to find them when the recording starts. Look at the parts that are already labelled or any headings as they may be mentioned.

✏ EXAM TASK

4 🎧 Look at the questions from Section 3 of a Listening test. Before listening, read the questions carefully, and decide what type of word(s) fits in each gap. Then listen and answer questions 1–6.

*Write **NO MORE THAN THREE WORDS** in each gap.*

Lecture Series

Recommended speaker: Dr Sally Martin

Most well-known book: **1** ....

Describes research into **2** ....

Subjects of lecture are **3** .... and space exploration

Work described as **4** ....

Professor Peter Vent: talk on physics

Works at the **5** .... in Washington

Talk will be **6** ....

5 Check your answers. Were your predictions about word-class correct?

60 mins

How to ... approach multiple-choice questions

1   **Look at the headline and introductory text. Without looking at the article, discuss in pairs which of these points you expect the article to talk about. (There are no right answers!)**

a) the importance of pollination

b) the health benefits of honey

c) the global decline in bee numbers

d) different honey varieties

e) the invention of the first beehive

f) how to treat a bee sting

Getting a **buzz** out of **bees**

The ancient art of beekeeping is making a comeback in the UK.

2   **Read the article once through. How many of these points were discussed?**

The pastime shared by Aristotle, Tolstoy, Sir Edmund Hillary and Sherlock Holmes has brought an excited buzz to Britain's suburbs and countryside. The British bee population has declined at an alarming rate over the last few years – by a third since 2007. There's also been a massive decline in the number of bee hives in the UK – nearly 75 per cent in the past century. However, there are signs of a resurgence in interest in the art of beekeeping.

Honey is perhaps the most remarkable of all foodstuffs. When enjoying this everyday treat, it rarely occurs to us that we are eating nectar gathered by bees and transformed by regurgitation into syrup that has the same sweetness as granulated sugar. A pound of clover honey requires nectar from eight million flowers. Over its lifetime (around thirty days in the summer months), a single worker bee will produce approximately

one-twelfth of a teaspoon of honey. It is just as well that the average population of a hive is 60,000 in summer.

The benefits of beekeeping are not merely culinary. For centuries, beeswax candles provided light. Mead was once the main source of intoxication. Even today, UK growers of apples, strawberries, oilseed rape and other crops depend on these ceaselessly toiling workers for cross-pollination. Humanity has been harvesting honey from the provident bee for at least 10,000 years. Bees hoard honey as a source of energy for the winter months and we steal their stores. Just like the suburban beekeeper with his smoke bellows, the Akie people of northern Tanzania use smouldering grass to pacify the wild bee swarms located high in baobab trees. Hives have been in use at least since ancient Egypt. The Roman poet Virgil wrote a comprehensive treatise on beekeeping.

In her book *The Hive*, the appropriately named Bee Wilson reveals that the British were eating about two kilos of honey per person per year by the 12th century. The arrival of sugar from Arab countries and the American slave plantations replaced our honey habit, though it enjoyed a small resurgence with the invention of the movable-frame hive by the Rev Lorenzo Langstroth in Philadelphia in 1860. His ingenious construction meant that the man-made hives no longer had to be destroyed in order to get the honey. The honeycomb, described by Bee Wilson as 'one of those natural phenomenons so marvellous that it is hard for us to believe they weren't made by human hands', is spun on a centrifuge to extract the honey before being restored to the hive. Sadly, such ingenuity did not restore the mass appeal of honey. Reports indicate that the British eat a mere half-jar per year compared with a gruesome 53 kilos of refined sugar. The heat treatment that ensures the liquidity of the cheap honey available in supermarkets also kills most of the subtle elements in the taste and the health benefits too.

Many people swear by the health properties of honey. Honey appears to be more effective in healing sore throats and coughs than proprietary medicines. Honey from the New Zealand manuka bush is said to be effective when used externally as a wound treatment and internally for digestive problems.

One of the pleasures of gaining a taste for honey is the vast range available. Those with expensive tastes may relish the honey from hives on the roof of the Paris Opera sold by the posh French grocers Fauchon or Fortnum & Mason's

honey from hives in the shadow of London Bridge. From his Hawaiian retreat, novelist Paul Theroux produces a honey called Oceania Ranch. Varieties sold by the Hive Honey Shop of Clapham, south-west London, suit all budgets and range from 'delicate' Wimbledon runny honey and 'fresh piquant' sainfoin red clover honey to 'very aromatic' ling heather honey and the 'bitter dark chocolate' flavour of autumn harvest honey.

For apiarist Philippa O'Brien, observing a colony is fascinating. 'You get very attached to bees,' she says. But it's not just about hazy summer days and sampling your own honey. O'Brien recommends beekeeping only if you go on a course to learn about bee management. 'Last winter was so cold and long that many of my

bees died,' she adds. 'Unless you feed your bees, they can starve. I feed them on sugar in autumn and fondant icing in winter. You need to know how to control the diseases and pests that have recently come in from the Far East. Our native bees can't deal with them. That's why there are no more wild bees in Britain. Feral colonies won't last more than eighteen months. You also need to know how to position your hives so that bees will fly in the right direction and not sting people. If they're not handled properly, bees can kill. Someone likened beekeeping to keeping a lion tied up in your garden. That's a bit of an exaggeration, but it's important that people go into beekeeping with their eyes open.'

_____ ▪

3a **Read the sentence stem and the four options for multiple-choice question 1 below. Then work in pairs and answer questions a) to d).**

> *Choose the correct letter, **A**, **B**, **C** or **D**.*
>
> **1** According to Philippa O'Brien,
>
>   **A** there are too many inexperienced beekeepers.
>
>   **B** there are serious issues to consider before taking up beekeeping.
>
>   **C** winter conditions pose the biggest problem for beekeepers.
>
>   **D** the risks of beekeeping are misrepresented.

a) Highlight the part of the passage this question refers to.

b) Does the question ask you to look for specific information or a general understanding of this part of the text?

c) Reread the section. Are there any answers you know are not correct? Why not?

d) Read the section one more time. Which answer is correct? Why?

3b **Now answer questions a) to d) for multiple-choice question 2.**

> *Choose the correct letter, **A**, **B**, **C** or **D**.*
>
> **2** What do the eating habits of British people suggest about granulated sugar?
>
>   **A** Quantities of sugar consumed are not as high as has been reported.
>
>   **B** White sugar is a better sweetener than honey.
>
>   **C** The taste of sugar is destroyed by processing.
>
>   **D** Table sugar is the preferred sweetener in the UK.

Boost your score!

Which key words in these questions will help you find the right place in the text? Underline them.

✎ EXAM TASK

4   **Now answer these multiple-choice questions about the same passage.**

Questions 3–8

*Choose the correct letter, **A**, **B**, **C** or **D**.*

3   In the first paragraph the writer makes the point that

   A   looking after bees is a worthwhile interest.

   B   problems for the UK bee population are ongoing.

   C   celebrity interest in keeping bees inspires others.

   D   current enthusiasm for beekeeping will be short-lived.

4   In the second paragraph, the writer states that

   A   producing honey is labour-intensive for the insects.

   B   consumers of honey are aware of how it is made.

   C   nectar-producing blooms are in short supply.

   D   honey has a more subtle taste than refined sugar.

5   The writer refers to beekeepers in Tanzania to exemplify the fact that

   A   caring for bees is a challenging pastime.

   B   beekeepers worldwide use hives for keeping bees.

   C   beekeepers in different parts of the world employ similar methods.

   D   some cultures are more knowledgeable about beekeeping than others.

6   Bee Wilson's research states that Langstroth's beehive

   A   had a lasting effect on the popularity of beekeeping.

   B   was based on the structure of honeycomb.

   C   replaced an earlier hive design.

   D   led to the destruction of old-fashioned hives.

7   What conclusion does the writer draw from the array of different honeys on sale?

   A   The best-tasting honey comes from rural locations.

   B   Higher priced honey has a more subtle flavour.

   C   The different honeys on sale do not vary much in taste.

   D   The variety of tastes is part of the attraction of honey.

8   Philippa O'Brien implies that

   A   bees from the Far East need to be controlled.

   B   many native bee species have been wiped out.

   C   honey-producing bees in the UK are farmed.

   D   bees are prone to pests and disease.

Boost your score!

Multiple-choice questions test several different reading skills. First, isolate the part of the reading passage which is being tested. Remember questions may focus on a general understanding of the main points or detailed understanding of specific points.

How to ... organise an essay

1a **Look at the following Task 2 question.**

> Nowadays the number of people living alone is higher than in the past.
>
> What are the reasons for this?
>
> Does this development have more advantages or disadvantages for society?

Give reasons for your answer and include any relevant examples from your own knowledge or experience.

1b **Read two sample answers, Essay A and Essay B. What is the main topic of each paragraph? What differences can you identify in the organisation of A and B?**

ESSAY A

In recent years, the amount of people who live on their own has steadily increased. There are several reasons for this development, as well as a number of advantages and disadvantages.

Firstly, a key reason for people living alone is the fact that marriage is less popular than before. Fewer people live with a family, and as the population goes up, there are more people living alone. A second reason may be advances in ways of communicating. People who live alone do not need to feel lonely, as we can all keep in touch easily with mobile phones, video messaging and social media. Furthermore, changes to the economy in many countries mean that more people can afford to live alone.

In terms of the effects on society, there are several advantages, such as people feeling more independent. Living alone means choosing your own lifestyle, without making compromises. Those who do not have a family to support may also spend more money in their local economy, which is a positive result for some areas. However, living alone could also lead to loneliness. In addition to this, people without a family to look after them will be more dependent on the state if they fall ill or need help.

To sum up, there are pros and cons to people living alone, but in my view, the advantages are greater than the disadvantages. Society needs young people who can put money back in to the economy, and this is a positive effect of this development.

ESSAY B

Recently, there has been an increase in the number of people living alone. There are several reasons for this development, and in my opinion, the advantages outweigh the disadvantages for society.

One of the main advantages of people living alone is that they can feel more independent. Living alone means choosing your own lifestyle, without making compromises. A second advantage is the fact that people who do not have a family to support may spend more money in their local economy, which is a positive result for some areas, and young people in particular are more likely to socialise and take part in public life.

On the other hand, there are some disadvantages. People living alone may be more dependent on the state if they fall ill or need help, for example. There may also be a negative impact on the environment, as several people living alone use more energy than a household of people sharing.

With regard to the reasons for this development, one is the fact that marriage is less popular than before. Fewer people live with a family, and as the population goes up, there are more people living alone. A second reason may be advances in ways of communicating. People who live alone do not need to feel lonely, as we can all keep in touch easily with mobile phones, video messaging and social media. Furthermore, changes to the economy in many countries mean that more people can afford to live alone.

To sum up, there are pros and cons to living alone, but I believe it is clear that there are more advantages than disadvantages.

1c **Work in pairs to check your ideas. Which style of essay do you prefer?**

2a **Read another Task 2 question.**

> *Some people think it is better to live in a big city, while others believe there are more advantages to living in the countryside.*
>
> *What is your opinion about this?*

Give reasons for your answer and include any relevant examples from your own knowledge or experience.

Look at a student's notes for this task. Group the ideas in a logical way and decide how to organise them into paragraphs.

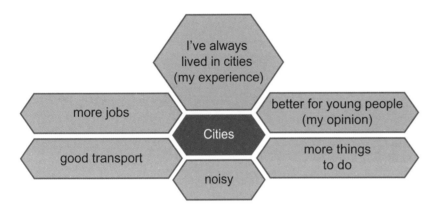

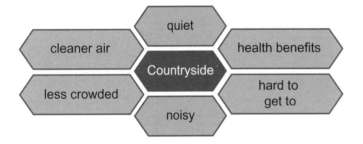

2b **Read the following sample answer. Are the paragraphs organised in the same way as your plan?**

Most people have a clear opinion about whether it is better to live in a city or in the countryside. I have always lived in cities, which is why I think living in a city has the most advantages. However, there are also many positives to living in the countryside.

Cities are busy and exciting places with plenty of things to do. If you have a hobby such as singing, playing a sport or drama, it is easy to join clubs and do these activities in a city. There are more jobs available and transport is more efficient. People who live in rural areas usually need a car to get around, as there are less train stations and buses.

Many people prefer to live in the countryside. It is usually quiet and peaceful, which is attractive to some people. There are some health benefits: cleaner air and a less stressful lifestyle, and the cost of living is often lower outside of city centres. Furthermore, the countryside is less crowded, which means it can be easier to find schools for children.

There are many pros and cons to both the city and the countryside, and the choice of where to live depends on personal preference. In my opinion, the city may be more suitable for younger people, and families may prefer to live in the countryside.

> **Boost your score!**
>
> To achieve a band 7 or above, each paragraph needs to have a clear central topic. Take a few minutes to plan how to organise your answer and decide what the topic of each paragraph will be before you start writing.

3a Look at the sample answer from exercise 2b again, this time with gaps. Write one appropriate linking expression from the box in each gap. Number 1 has been done as an example.

> in contrast ~~personally~~ in addition to sum up for example
> whereas to begin with nevertheless

Most people have a clear opinion about whether it is better to live in a city or in the countryside. (**1**) _____Personally_____, I have always lived in cities, which is why I think living in a city has the most advantages. However, there are also many positives to living in the countryside.

(**2**) _____, cities are busy and exciting places with plenty of things to do. If you have a hobby such as singing, playing a sport or drama, it is easy to join clubs and do these activities in a city. (**3**) _____, there are more jobs available and transport is more efficient. (**4**) _____, people who live in rural areas usually need a car to get around, as there are less train stations and buses.

(**5**) _____, many people prefer to live in the countryside. It is usually quiet and peaceful, which is attractive to some people. There are some health benefits, (**6**) _____ cleaner air and a less stressful lifestyle, and the cost of living is often lower outside of city centres. Furthermore, the countryside is less crowded, which means it can be easier to find schools for children.

(**7**) _____, there are many pros and cons to both the city and the countryside, and the choice of where to live depends on personal preference. In my opinion, the city may be more suitable for younger people, (**8**) _____ families may prefer to live in the countryside.

3b Match the linkers from the box with synonyms below. An example has been done for you.

1	nevertheless	**a)**	while
2	in contrast	**b)**	for instance
3	personally	**c)**	in conclusion
4	in addition	**d)**	contrastingly
5	to sum up	**e)**	however
6	for example	**f)**	first
7	whereas	**g)**	in my experience
8	to begin with	**h)**	furthermore

(1 nevertheless — e) however)

Boost your score!

To achieve a band 7 or above in Task 2, ideas need to be logically organised, using a range of cohesive devices appropriately. However, using too many linkers in a way that is confusing could actually reduce your score, so aim to use them to guide the reader through your essay.

✎ EXAM TASK

4 **Complete the writing task.**

You should spend about 40 minutes on this task.

Write about the following topic:

> *In recent years, international tourism has become more and more popular, with an increase in the number of people who travel abroad for holidays.*
>
> *What are the reasons for this? Do you think this is a positive or negative development?*

Give reasons for your answer and include any relevant examples from your own knowledge or experience.

Write at least 250 words.

How to ... organise a discussion

1a Questions a–e are examples of questions asked by an examiner in Part 3 of the Speaking test. Match questions a–e with the question functions i)–v).

a) What do you think about older people living in care homes?

b) What are the differences between family life nowadays and in the past?

c) How do you think family life could change in the future?

d) Why do so many parents wait until they are older to have children these days?

e) Some people say the government has a responsibility to look after older people. What do you think?

i) agree or disagree

ii) speculate

iii) compare

iv) explain

v) give opinion

1b Listen to a candidate answering the questions above. Match the answers to the questions.

1 ....   2 ....   3 ....   4 ....   5 ....

1c Look at the transcript on page 123 and listen again. As you listen, <u>underline</u> any useful discourse markers you hear.

1d Work in pairs and discuss.

a) Which expressions from the transcript were used to:

- agree?
- speculate?
- make comparisons?

b) Can you add any more expressions for the same functions?

1e Work in pairs. Discuss the following questions. Try to include some of the discourse markers you underlined.

a) What are the differences between working life nowadays and in the past?

b) What do you think about doing voluntary work if paid work is hard to find?

c) How do you think working life could change in the future?

d) Why do some people prefer to work from home?

e) Some people say that getting good qualifications at school is essential for future job success – what's your opinion?

2a Listen to three candidates answering the question below. Which is the best answer? Why?

How important do you think it is for children not to watch too much TV?

2b Look at the following Part 3 questions. Think of at least two points to make about each one.

a) What can be done to encourage people to eat more healthily?

Example: *tax on unhealthy foods*

....

....

....

b) How important is it for children to learn to cook at school?

....

....

c) Do people from your country have a healthy diet in general?

....

....

d) Why do some people enjoy eating in restaurants?

....

....

e) How do you think people's eating habits might change in the future?

....

....

> **Boost your score!**
>
> While in Parts 1 and 2 you speak about personal information and experiences, the questions in Part 3 are more abstract. You will be expected to discuss a range of issues and ideas in detail. Try to think about each question from positive and negative points of view if appropriate, and aim to give more than one example or reason.

2c Work in pairs. Discuss the questions together. Did you have similar ideas?

✏ EXAM TASK

3a Work in pairs.

Student A: You are the examiner. Ask your partner the questions. Listen carefully to your partner and check they use discourse markers.

Student B: You are the candidate. Listen and answer the question. Remember to give full answers and use discourse markers.

> **A** Let's talk about transport:
>
> What types of transport are used most regularly in your country? Why?
>
> How important is it for a country to have an efficient system of public transport? Why?
>
> What changes might there be to transport in the next fifty years? Why?

3b Change roles.

Student B: You are the examiner. Ask your partner the questions. Listen carefully to your partner and check they use discourse markers.

Student A: You are the candidate. Listen and answer the question. Remember to give full answers and use discourse markers.

> **B** Let's talk about travel:
>
> What do you think children can learn from travelling widely?
>
> How have the holidays that people take changed over the last fifty years?
>
> Some people say that flying should be more expensive because of the damage it does to the environment – what is your opinion?

LISTENING

Make a photocopy of the Listening test answer sheet on page 108.

 SECTION 1

Questions 1–10

Complete the notes below.

*Write **ONE WORD AND/OR A NUMBER** for each answer.*

THINK IT THROUGH

It is essential to read each question carefully before you listen. Decide what type of word or words are needed (noun, adjective, verb phrase, etc.) and check the answer fits grammatically with the words around it.

 What type of information will be in this gap?

Work Experience

Place of work	Main duties	Hours of work	Other details
Example: (0) .... shop	Serving customers	Mainly 1	Should be confident Start this 2 ....
3	4 .... assistant	11am – 3pm Mondays to Wednesdays	Located near the 5 .... No experience needed
Hotel	Helping the 6	7 .... a week	Essential to arrive on time for work
8	9 .... duties	12pm – 5pm Monday to Friday	Must be 10 ....

 What part of speech will the word in this gap be?

 **SECTION 2**

Questions 11–13

Choose **THREE** *letters,* **A–G**.

Which **THREE** activities are available for children to try?

11 ....

12 ....

13 ....

Dalbree Family Festival	
A	Football skills
B	Climbing
C	Archery
D	Dance workshop
E	Arts and crafts
F	Tennis coaching
G	Cookery class

Questions 14–20

Write **ONE WORD ONLY** *for each answer.*

Family Festival Programme for Sunday		
Place	**Event**	**Details**
Mini Arena	Poetry reading	• takes place until **14** ....
Cafe Tent	Food stalls and space for **15**	• good prices on **16** ...., rolls and ice cream
Stage	Theatre performances	• information will be on a **17** .... • come 10 minutes before start
Music Zone	Various bands and singers	• no **18** .... allowed
Long field	Sports competitions	• including long jump and a variety of **19** ....
Gallery	Display of work by **20** .... artists	• many pieces available to buy

SECTION 3

Questions 21–24

 Complete the sentences below.

*Write **NO MORE THAN TWO WORDS** for each answer.*

Young People and Technology

21   The project focuses on young people who are ....

22   Rob and Emma have plenty of data about ....

23   They are going to do .... to collect extra information.

24   Rob and Emma need to do more work on their .... next.

Questions 25–30

*Choose the correct letter **A**, **B** or **C**.*

25   How did a minority of people say they would feel if they lost their mobile phone?
     A   It would make them worry about missing something.
     B   It would make them feel relieved.
     C   It would make little difference to them.

26   What was the main reason most young people gave for carrying a mobile phone?
     A   to communicate important information
     B   to keep in touch with friends
     C   to have access to the internet

27   Compared with their parents, young people today tend to spend
     A   more time on their homework.
     B   less time on their homework.
     C   the same amount of time on their homework.

28   Why do Rob and Emma include an example of having an idea in the shower?
     A   It shows that hot water can wake us up.
     B   It shows that people often think best in the morning.
     C   It shows that having a clear head helps creativity.

29   Rob and Emma are both surprised to find out
     A   how often young people check their phones.
     B   the number of texts some people send.
     C   the amount of time people spend looking at a screen.

30   What does Emma enjoy about getting a new message on her phone?
     A   It is a distraction from daily life.
     B   It makes her feel that she has a lot of friends.
     C   It presents the possibility of something exciting.

 **SECTION 4**

Questions 31–40

Complete the notes below.

*Write **NO MORE THAN THREE WORDS** for each answer.*

Flight compensation

Case study

Recent flight with Bolt Airlines

People discussed the flight on **31** ....

First problem

    – passengers were unable to **32** ....

    – delayed for 5 hours

Second problem

    – return flight then had a fault with the **33** ....

    – plane could not take off when the airport was **34** ....

    – no staff available due to a **35** ....

Third problem

    – further delay when flight crew were involved in a **36** ....

Passengers eventually took off 30 hours late

Rules of compensation

The amount of compensation varies according to **37** .... as well as the length of the delay.

Meals must be provided if the delay is **38** ....

Compensation is unlikely if a flight is cancelled for certain reasons such as **39** ....

Claiming compensation online is so complex that people **40** ....

> You will be given ten minutes at the end of the test to transfer your answers to the answer sheet.

READING

Make a photocopy of the Reading test answer sheet on page 109.

READING PASSAGE 1

*You should spend about 20 minutes on **Questions 1–13**, which are based on Reading Passage 1 below.*

THINK IT THROUGH

Keep an eye on the time. There are three reading texts and forty questions to answer in one hour. Don't spend more than twenty minutes on each reading passage and tasks. If you really can't answer a question, leave it and come back to it if there is time at the end of the test.

Devils Fight Back

After a decades-long battle with a deadly disease, Tasmanian devils may now have a chance at survival

Tasmanian devils have been the top predators on the Australian island of Tasmania for more than a century. They were named by early European settlers because of their ferocious sounding screeches and reputed bad temper. It was this aggressive behaviour that made them so notorious that farmers were encouraged to shoot them until 1941. But for the past twenty years, the furry, cat-size creatures have been under attack for a different reason. A deadly disease has been threatening the animals' existence so conservationists have been working hard to save the dying species. Contrary to the predictions, today's devils seem to be fighting back. Now scientists think the endangered animals may be combatting the disease on their own.

Tasmanian devils suffer from an illness known as devil facial tumour disease (DFTD). First discovered in Tasmania in 1996, DFTD spread across the island so quickly that scientists predicted the species would be wiped out in a matter of decades. It causes massive lumps to form around a devil's face, and as they swell they often break and bleed, leaving the devil badly disfigured. As time passes these can prevent the animal from eating and breathing, and the illness is almost always fatal. 'The sheer number of animals that don't survive is overwhelming,' says David Pemberton, manager of the Save the Tasmanian Devil Programme.

Devils are found only in Tasmania and they're known for their ferocious-sounding screeches. The animals are the world's largest carnivorous marsupial, meat eaters whose babies finish developing in pouches outside their mothers' wombs. Devils are also one of only three types of animals, including dogs, known to be susceptible to a *transmissible cancer*, like DFTD. These cancers can pass between animals of the same species.

Normally cancer isn't contagious but when devils come into close contact with one another – through biting, for example – a sick animal can transmit DFTD cells to a healthy one. By 2011, DFTD had wiped out more than half of the wild devils so conservationists were making plans in case the animals became extinct. 'At that point, we were prepared to repopulate wild populations using individuals we were breeding in captivity, since they were the only animals who hadn't been exposed to the disease,' says Pemberton.

By early 2016, however, it was clear that the devils weren't vanishing as fast as experts had feared. Most of the animals that caught the disease eventually succumbed to it but some lived longer than others. A few of these devils resisted the disease long enough to reproduce and pass on their genes before they died. Scientists wondered if there might be something special about the offspring of these more-resistant devils. 'When a disease wipes out 80% of the individuals in a population, you expect the remaining population to be somehow genetically different,' explains Paul Hohenlohe, an evolutionary geneticist at the University of Idaho. Their studies showed that a small number of the animals carry genes that may make them resistant to the disease.

In the evolutionary process known as *natural selection*, animals that are better adapted to their environment survive to produce more offspring. This process usually takes place very slowly. Devils though, are changing more rapidly than normal, spreading DFTD resistant genes through the population in as few as four to six generations. As these genes proliferate through the Tasmanian devil population, its genetic make-up appears to be quickly evolving.

The devils' rapid evolution may be the key to their rebound. In late 2016, researchers made a remarkable discovery: for the first time, some devils were actually recovering from the disease. Scientists saw these recoveries as further proof that genetic changes and natural selection are allowing wild devils to evolve and overcome the disease naturally. One day breeding programmes may be able to encourage disease-resistant traits in Tasmanian devils to help the genes of the more resilient animals spread through the wild populations. These promising recoveries have also lead scientists to believe that a vaccine might be effective in helping the devils beat the cancer.

Despite this good news for the devils, new complications are beginning to emerge. A second strain of transmissible cancer, called devil facial tumour 2 (DFT2), was discovered in devils in southeastern Tasmania. Scientists don't know much about this illness yet, and they're not sure what effects the disease will have. But, according to Pemberton, devils are tough creatures. Plus, the people of Tasmania won't let their most iconic animal slip away without a fight. 'Tasmanians love their devils,' he says, 'and they will do anything to bring them back from the brink of extinction.'

Questions 1–7

Do the following statements agree with the information given in Reading Passage 1?

In boxes 1–7 on your answer sheet, write

TRUE *if the statement agrees with the information*
FALSE *if the statement contradicts the information*
NOT GIVEN *if there is no information on this*

1   Tasmanian devils were protected by early European settlers.

2   Tasmanian devils sometimes eat household pets.

3   Female devils carrying babies have the highest rates of DFTD.

4   Tasmanian devils can catch DFTD from biting each other.

5   Some Tasmanian devils carry a gene which prevents them from catching DFTD.

6   No Tasmanian devils have survived DFTD.

7   DFT2 is more dangerous than the original DFTD disease.

THINK IT THROUGH

Remember that the True / False / Not Given questions will not use exactly the same words as in the passage. Some words may be the same, but the rest will be **paraphrased**.

For example, in sentence 5, 'carry a gene which prevents them from catching DFTD' is a paraphrase for 'may make them resistant to the disease' in the fifth paragraph of the passage.

Questions that are false will **explicitly contradict** the information in the passage and may use antonyms or phrases that mean the opposite, e.g. the focus of question 6 is whether any devils survive the illness. Compare the sentence in question 6 with the information in the second paragraph in the passage which says that 'the illness is almost always fatal'.

Questions 8–13

Complete the sentences below.

*Choose **ONE WORD ONLY** from the passage for each answer.*

8 A Tasmanian devil that has DFTD gets large growths on

its ....

9 DFTD can make feeding **difficult** for the animals and can

also stop them from ....

This question asks you to look for the difficulties DFTD causes devils. The first is given (feeding). Can you find another?

10 Tasmanian devils are like .... because they can

both be affected by a type of cancer which can be caught from

another animal.

11 After 80% of Tasmanian devils had died from DFTD, scientists

assumed the survivors had changed ....

12 Tasmanian devils displayed signs of evolutionary change

within four ....

13 Scientists hope to protect the animals by developing

a .... which can be given to the animals

to stop the disease.

When you read this sentence, a possible answer could be 'years' or 'decades'. Find a time reference in the text saying how long it takes for this change to happen.

THINK IT THROUGH

Sentence completion

All the missing words can be found in the text. Check if the word is singular or plural and what part of speech it is. For example, both 'face' (noun) and 'facial' (adjective) appear in the text but which is the correct part of speech for Question 8? Copy the word from the text carefully so your spelling is correct.

READING PASSAGE 2

*You should spend about 20 minutes on **Questions 14–27**, which are based on Reading Passage 2 below.*

The Commodore 64

The iconic computer's influence should alter how we teach the next generation

A Back in 1982, starting up your home computer didn't come with soothing chimes and airbrushed icons. Operating an 8-bit machine was a voyage of discovery, characterized by repeated stabs in the dark and precious little hand-holding. The Commodore 64, arguably the best-selling computer model of all time, presented you with a blue screen and the message '38911 BASIC BYTES FREE. READY.' Ready for what? Ready for code. Clacking away at the keyboard in a language the machine understood (in this case BASIC) was the only means by which you could interact with it.

B It seems almost laughable today as we point, click, swipe and pinch our way through rich graphical user interfaces, but the user-unfriendliness of the Commodore 64 and its cousins taught a generation of enthusiasts how to program. 'It was the dawn of a new age,' says Jeff Minter, a legendary games programmer whose reputation was cemented by his work for the Commodore 64. 'It opened up worlds of creativity to people who otherwise might never have found them.'

C The Commodore 64 debuted at the Consumer Electronics Show in Las Vegas in January 1982 to gasps of disbelief from competing technology firms. Its graphic and sonic capabilities seemed way beyond its $595 price tag, and when it became available in the US in August that year, it quickly trounced the opposition. An aggressive marketing campaign saw it appear on the shelves of toy and department stores, contributing to a steep decline in the popularity of games consoles – but while gaming was its main selling point, you could do so much more. 'There was a huge enthusiasm for coding back then, for pushing the limits of the machine,' says one former Commodore 64 owner, Steve Harcourt. 'It was relatively easy to code for, and there were a vast amount of details available about its internal structure.' It may well have been cutting-edge, but you could become familiar with its every intricacy if you were willing to put the hours in. And many people were. 'The distance between the people who made the games and the people playing them wasn't that big,' says Minter. 'It was the spirit of independence. The programmers were a lot like you.'

D Minter's games for the Commodore 64, such as *Attack of the Mutant Camels* and *Sheep in Space*, were ground-breaking and hugely popular but he was also just one member of a burgeoning Commodore 64 community. Compunet, an early British interactive service accessed through a Commodore 64 and a painfully slow modem, brought that community closer together. 'It offered chat rooms and software downloads,' says Harcourt. 'This encouraged us to code, and it inspired a deeper enthusiasm for the machine beyond casual gaming.'

E That eagerness to outdo each other, coupled with the limitations of the machine itself, encouraged truly creative programming. It's notable that during the wave of nostalgia generated by the 30th anniversaries of the Commodore 64, the BBC Micro and other machines, the people who learned to program in the early 1980s are all thankful for being in the right place at the right time. 'I taught myself BBC Basic, and by the time I was 15 I was writing programs like disc sector editors,' says IT consultant Simon Guerrero. 'Even if you were just playing games you had to acquire at least a basic understanding of operating system (OS) operations – but now all you have to do is choose menu options.'

F   An awareness of the growing ignorance of computer languages is behind a number of initiatives to spark curiosity in what's going on under the bonnet of modern computers. Making programming accessible to people is vital but it's going to be an uphill battle to reignite an interest in coding that was probably at its peak thirty years ago, when machines like the Commodore 64 just sat there awaiting instructions. 'The link between code and creativity is one I think we should really emphasise, and one that we seem to have lost a bit,' says Hannah Dee, lecturer in computer science at Aberystwyth University. But in an age where our computers require no understanding of underlying architecture or components, and computer science is still considered to be a deeply uncool subject in comparison to arts and media, how will a new generation of computer wizards discover their true calling? 'If you want to play with programming,' says Dee, 'there are ways and means of doing it on any old computer – you can start web programming with Internet Explorer and Notepad.'

Questions 14–18

Complete the summary below.

Choose ONE WORD ONLY from the passage for each answer.

Write your answers in boxes 14–18 on your answer sheet.

Features of the Commodore 64

Unlike the interfaces on modern computers, the Commodore 64 didn't welcome users with calming tones or stylized **14** .... It used a simple coded language called **15** ...*BA*............. but it was not easy to use. The fact that it was so difficult to use meant many users learnt the skills they needed to **16** .... it. When it was launched, it was considered to be good value due to its superior sound and **17** .... capacity. Initially it was sold mainly for **18** ...., although it had many other potential applications.

Questions 19–23

Look at the following statements (Questions 19–23) and the list of people below.

*Match each statement with the correct person, **A–F**.*

*Write the correct letter, **A–F**, in boxes 19–23 on your answer sheet.*

NB   *You may use any letter more than once.*

19   People could learn from the machine even when they were using it for fun.

20   Users only need basic equipment to learn how to program.

21   Without the Commodore 64, some people might not have discovered their creativity.

22   The relationship between coding and imagination has diminished.

23   People wanted to use the machine to its full capacity.

List of people
A   Minter
B   Harcourt
C   Guerrero
D   Dee

THINK IT THROUGH

Underline the names of the people in the passage and try to find differences between what each of them says. Then read the sentences and match them to the names of the people.

Questions 24–27

Reading Passage 2 has seven paragraphs, **A–G**.

Which paragraph contains the following information?

*Write the correct letter, **A–G**, in boxes 24–27 on your answer sheet.*

NB You may use any letter more than once.

24 a reference to relationships which developed between Commodore 64 users

25 a mention of the negative reputation associated with computer studies

26 a description of how easy it is to navigate computer programs today

27 a claim that users are grateful they started programming in the 1980s

Boost your score!

Matching information

The information targeted in these questions will be found in more than one part of the text. Find references to the topic in all of the paragraphs and decide which one is **closest** in meaning to the information in the question.

1a Look at item 26. This has several pieces of key information: description, ease of using computer programs and today.

1b Look at paragraphs A–G again and answer the questions below.

a) Which two paragraphs mention computers **today**?

b) Which of these two paragraphs gives a **description** of using computers today?

c) Which of the two paragraphs provides the better answer for item 26?

1c Check your answers in the key.

READING PASSAGE 3

*You should spend about 20 minutes on **Questions 28–40**, which are based on Reading Passage 3 below.*

The Passages of Herman Melville

A review of the biographic novel by Jay Parini

Herman Melville (1819–1891) was an American writer who was most famous for his novel *Moby Dick*. The truth about Melville remains as elusive as that great white whale chased in the story of *Moby Dick*. In one of his exquisite short stories 'Bartleby, the Scrivener', Herman Melville writes of his protagonist that 'no materials exist for a full and satisfactory biography of this man'. And so it is with Melville himself. Posterity lifted the author of *Moby Dick* to the ranks of America's greatest writers, but he was overlooked in his own time, many of his letters and manuscripts are lost and there is much that remains open to conjecture.

Jay Parini's novel, *The Passages of Herman Melville*, aims to give us a clearer picture of the enigmatic 'H M', recreating episodes from his early adventures at sea to his final years as a struggling poet. Parini's historical fiction – he has previously written novels about the writers Tolstoy and Walter Benjamin – is based on his conviction that literary art can illuminate where conventional scholarship cannot: he has Melville observe that 'only novels tell the unadorned truth'. He explores aspects of Melville's life that remain beyond the reach of biographers: the subtleties of his relationship with his wife, Lizzie; the depth of his frustration at the commercial failure of his books; the complicated undercurrent to his friendship with Amercian author Nathaniel Hawthorne.

The first half of the novel describes Melville's experiences as a somewhat risky young sailor. Parini recounts how, on a whaling voyage in the Pacific in 1842, Melville jumped ship and lived among a tribe of cannibals on the island of Nuku Hiva before escaping to Hawaii to join the crew of an American frigate bound for home. It is a thrilling tale, but Parini's account feels redundant; after all, Melville published two very readable books – *Typee* and *Omoo* – about his time in Polynesia, and one might as well consult the man himself. However, this period of Melville's life was crucial to his writing, as Parini explains:

> Now, for the first time, Herman began to think about the nature of fiction, and how it so often depended upon, even hugged, reality, embracing true stories…Herman realized with a shudder of quiet pleasure that what occurred here, aboard the Acushnet, might find itself one day in a work of fiction by his own hand. He knew it would, and vowed to listen keenly, to watch and record in his journal whatever transpired, collecting snippets of conversation, images, phrases, ideas for tales, moods, inklings, omens. (pp. 75–76)

Another problem with these chapters is Parini's tendency to speculate about where Melville picked up these ideas for the rich, philosophical fiction he penned in the 1850s. Bartleby's famous remark 'I prefer not to' is spoken by a recalcitrant shipmate on an early cruise ('the phrase etched itself in Herman Melville's brain'), while *Moby Dick's* Captain Ahab springs from the tale of a monomaniac whaling captain overheard one night on deck ('the narrative sunk deep in Herman's memory'). This crude approach gives the false impression that Melville – possessed of perhaps the most powerful imagination in American literature – was simply a talented magpie.

Parini is better when he turns to the later years. The account of Melville's all-too-brief career as a writer, before the steady decline into obscurity, is delicate and convincing. And when Parini appraises the work, he has the knack for finding just the right phrase, as when he refers to Melville's 'iron whimsicality': a more definitive description of his singular prose style you will not find. The image of Melville as an old man, after he had given up fiction and taken a job in a New York customs house, is beautifully drawn: 'He had lived a thousand lives thus far ... in a way, he was already posthumous, ghosting the streets, watching and listening.' This haunting image of Melville remains long after the book is read.

But while there is much to admire in this novel, it only deepens the mystery of Melville. The narrative is told partly in Lizzie's voice and partly in the third person, which means that we must rely on dialogue for glimpses of Melville's inner life. Unfortunately he is curiously reticent, offering only the odd gnomic utterance ('What lies beyond interests me'; 'We can't see ourselves without stories'). As a result, Melville remains, like the white whale of his great novel, *Moby Dick*, elusive to the last.

Questions 28–31

*Choose the correct letter, **A**, **B**, **C** or **D**.*

Write the correct letter in boxes 28–31 on your answer sheet.

28 In the first paragraph, the writer says Melville's life remains a mystery because
  A people focus on *Moby Dick* at the expense of his other work.
  B there is a lack of information about Melville.
  C few biographies have been written about Melville in the past.
  D biographers failed to use some of the primary sources about Melville.

29 What is the writer's opinion of the first half of the novel?
  A It is an unnecessary repetition of Melville's own descriptions.
  B It is easier to read than Melville's own account of his life.
  C It fails to convey the excitement the author intended.
  D It contains interesting historical details.

30 What is the writer's opinion of Parini's interpretation of the quote 'I prefer not to'?
  A Parini's theories are overly creative.
  B Melville probably misquoted his original source.
  C Parini underestimates Melville's creativity.
  D Melville's originality is questionable.

Find the part of the text which discusses the 'false impression' that Parini gives of Melville's imaginative skills. Which option in question 30 paraphrases this idea?

31 What is the writer's main idea in the final paragraph?
  A Parini's biography uncovers secrets of Melville's life.
  B Melville would disagree with Parini's assessment of his life.
  C Parini has produced the finest biography of Melville yet.
  D Parini's biography creates more questions than it answers.

Questions 32–36

Do the following statements agree with the views/claims of the writer in Reading Passage 3?

In boxes 32–36 on your answer sheet, write

YES	if the statement agrees with the claims of the writer
NO	if the statement contradicts the claims of the writer
NOT GIVEN	if it is impossible to say what the writer thinks about this

32 Melville was underappreciated during his lifetime.

33 Parini's previous historical fiction is superior to this book.

34 Parini said Melville believed that fiction was more truthful than non-fiction.

35 Parini's account of Melville's Pacific voyage is exaggerated.

36 Melville's writing in the 1850s was unsatisfactory.

 THINK IT THROUGH

This task tests your understanding of the writer's opinions and ideas in the text.

Questions 37–40

Complete the summary using the list of words, **A–H**, below.

Write the correct letter, **A–H**, in boxes 37–40 on your answer sheet.

Melville's Later Years

The writer is impressed by Parini's account of Melville's writing career, and it is described as a

37 .... and also gentle representation of Melville's later life. Parini describes him as having an

'iron whimsicality' which the writer believes is a **38** .... explanation of Melville's style. Parini's

portrayal of his life in New York is elegantly written and **39** .... for the writer. However, Parini's

use of the Lizzie's voice as the narrator means it is difficult to know what Melville was thinking. The writer

concludes that both Melville and Moby Dick are **40** .... characters.

A precise	**B** sympathetic	**C** subtle
D artistic	**E** believable	**F** puzzling
G literal	**H** memorable	

WRITING

TASK 1

You should spend about 20 minutes on this task.

> The table and bar chart below give information about the percentage of the population owning a smartphone in eight different countries, and owners of smartphones by age group in the USA in 2014.
>
> Summarise the information by selecting and reporting the main features, and make comparisons where relevant.

Write at least 150 words.

Country	Percentage of population that owned a smartphone in 2014
Russia	36
United Arab Emirates	74
China	47
India	13
South Africa	40
USA	56

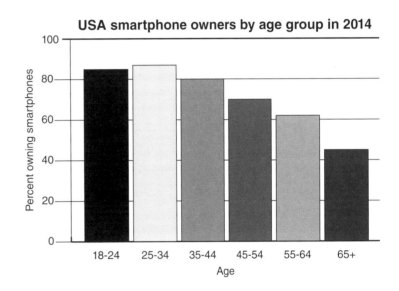

TASK 2

You should spend about 40 minutes on this task.

Write about the following topic:

> Nowadays it is becoming easier for anyone to become famous. Does this development have more advantages or disadvantages for individuals, and for society as a whole?

Give reasons for your answer and include any relevant examples from your own knowledge or experience.

Write at least 250 words.

SPEAKING

PART 1: Introduction and interview

Drawing and painting

- How often do you draw or paint a picture? Why?

- Do you enjoy looking at art in galleries or museums? Why? / Why not?

- Do you think children should learn to draw and paint at school? Why? / Why not?

- Would you ever buy a drawing or painting by someone else? Why? / Why not?

PART 2: Individual long turn

You will have to talk about the topic for one to two minutes.

You have one minute to think about what you are going to say.

You can make some notes to help you if you wish.

> Talk about a news story you read or heard about that made you happy.
>
> You should say
>
> > what the story was about
> >
> > how you found out about it
> >
> > when it happened
>
> and why it made you happy.

Final question

Do you usually pay attention to what is happening in the news?

PART 3: Two-way discussion

News around the world

How important is it for individuals to know about what is happening in the world? Why?

Is local news more important for individuals than global news? Why / Why not?

What is the best way to find out about local news?

Media controls

To what extent should we believe the news stories that are on the internet? Why?

Whose responsibility is it to ensure that we can trust news on TV and in newspapers? Why?

Boost your score!

🎧 3.3 – 🎧 3.5 Listen to Maria's Speaking test. Which of her answers do you think are particularly good? Why? Look at the transcripts on pages 126–128. Underline the linking phrases that Maria uses effectively.

PHOTOCOPIABLE

LISTENING

Make a photocopy of the Listening test answer sheet on page 108.

 SECTION 1

Questions 1–5

Complete the notes below.

Write **NO MORE THAN THREE WORDS AND/OR A NUMBER** *for each answer.*

Ordering office furniture

> *Example*
>
> David is a (**0**) ...sales assistant...

Office desk

design name: **1** .... desk

made of **2** ....

Size:

3 .... metres wide

53 cm deep

4 .... centimetres high

Matching **5** .... is available

Printer

Model number: **6** ....

Comes with **7** .... guarantee

Both items delivered together

Delivery date **8** ....

To find out delivery time **9** ....

Total cost **10** ....

 You will be given half a minute at the end of each section of the Listening test to check your answers.

 **SECTION 2**

Questions 11–15

Complete the notes below.

*Write **ONE WORD** for each answer.*

Community Classes

11 The drama class is particularly ....

12 Language lessons are suitable for ....

13 .... lessons have never been taught here before.

14 Students of singing lessons can participate in .... on a regular basis.

15 The first baking class will be ....

Questions 16–20

Complete the flow chart below.

*Write **ONE WORD AND / OR A NUMBER** for each answer.*

To attend a Community Class

Look at the timetable on the website and choose the class you would like to do.

⬇

Send an email to the **16** .... to find out whether places are available.

⬇

Check whether the course you want to do is linked with **17** ....

⬇

Pay a deposit of **18** .... to book your place.

⬇

You will receive a letter and a **19** .... in the post.

⬇

You must pay the full course fees **20** .... before the start date.

 SECTION 3

Questions 21–26

*Choose the correct letter, **A**, **B** or **C**.*

Presentation on coastal geography

21 What change has Patrick decided to make to his presentation?
    A   to make it longer
    B   to change the organisation of information
    C   to focus on a different sub-topic

22 What information does the tutor advise adding to the presentation?
    A   an illustration of two different types of waves
    B   a demonstration of the effects of high winds
    C   a specific example of one coastal area

23 Patrick decides to do further reading about
    A   acids contained in seawater.
    B   causes of cracks in cliffs.
    C   the differences between chalk and clay rock.

24 Why does the tutor think Patrick should speak to his classmates?
    A   because he needs help with his visual media
    B   because there is too much research for one person to do
    C   because they should avoid covering the same information

25 What problem has Patrick previously had when giving a class presentation?
    A   He spoke too quickly.
    B   He used technical vocabulary.
    C   His body language was poor.

26 What feedback does Patrick give about a recent seminar?
    A   He says the content was completely relevant to the course.
    B   He says the students enjoyed the collaborative element.
    C   He says it was presented in an interesting way.

Questions 27–30

Complete the notes below.

*Write **ONE WORD ONLY** for each answer.*

Field Trip

27 A minibus will leave at 9:30am from outside the ....

28 Students should bring a .... as well as a pencil and a notebook.

29 There will be a chance to analyse cliffs, beaches and ....

30 A coastal warden will be there to talk about a .... by the sea.

 **SECTION 4**

Questions 31–40

Complete the notes below.

*Write **ONE WORD ONLY** for each answer.*

Jasper Johns – American artist

<u>Young life</u>

First experience of art was seeing paintings by his **31** ....

Inspired by art in a local **32** ....

Unlike other artists, he believed art should be **33** ....

In his 20s, he decided to **34** .... his artwork

<u>Famous works</u>

Flag – painted on **35** ....

       paint mixed with **36** ....

Target – resembles an **37** ....

<u>Style</u>

Highlights his presence as the artist in his work

More than 180 of his works feature **38** ....

Does not produce paintings of **39** .... as they are too emotional

<u>Now</u>

Work from 1950s is still his most popular

Large-scale paintings are hard to purchase because they are **40** ....

 You will be given ten minutes at the end of the Listening test to transfer your answers to the answer sheet.

READING

Make a photocopy of the Reading test answer sheet on page 109.

READING PASSAGE 1

*You should spend about 20 minutes on **Questions 1–13**, which are based on Reading Passage 1 below.*

The Great Divide

The Rocky Mountains mark a geographical divide in North America.

Over one third of the state of Colorado is public property, a boundless wilderness with some of the finest mountain scenery in North America. The backbone of the state – indeed, of the whole continent – is the Rocky Mountains, which stretch some 2,700 miles from Alaska to Mexico. The present mountains were formed by the great forces of plate tectonics 70 million years ago, when the dinosaurs still roamed the earth. In fact, they are the third set of Rocky Mountains: two earlier and much older formations were thrust skywards and then eroded over many tens of millions of years. They say it's possible to cross the continental divide eleven times when journeying north to south through Colorado. This continental divide is the geographical watershed that separates the rivers that flow to the Pacific Ocean in the West from those that flow, ultimately, to the Atlantic in the East.

Two hours north of Denver is Estes Park, an impressive 7,522 feet above sea level and the entry point for the Rocky Mountain National Park. Although the Rocky Mountain National Park is only one-ninth the size of the better-known Yellowstone, it receives roughly the same number of visitors. Nevertheless, it is not difficult to find oneself in virtual solitude, even on some of the easier trails leading off from the road.

There are three distinct ecosystems in the park, delineated by altitude. The highest is the alpine tundra above the tree line between 11,500 feet and 14,000 feet. Here, small, waxy-leaved plants are adapted to the fierce drying winds, bitter cold and intense UV-rich sunlight. Below comes the sub-alpine area with its wind-driven huckleberry and juniper shrubs. The lowest is the montane region with its tall ponderosa and wispy aspen cloaked in shimmering, summer-green foliage. The overpowering scent is from older ponderosa, which develop a cinnamon-red bark that warms in the sunshine to fill the air with fragrance.

Breathlessness is a problem in Colorado's mountains, and not just because of the magnificence of the landscape. The highest peak in the entire Rockies is Colorado's Mount Elbert, at 14,440 feet. In the Rocky Mountain National Park, the highest is Longs Peak at 14,259 feet. Even at the 'lower' altitudes, anyone coming from sea level will soon feel the effects: fatigue, shortness of breath, headaches and a raking thirst.

Outside the city of Colorado Springs, it is possible to see the curiously shaped remnants of the Rockies' ancient geology in the form of a stunning rock formation in a city park called the Garden of the Gods. Some of these rocks date back 300 million years to the time of the first formation: the Ancient Rocky Mountains. Over a period of many hundreds of thousands of years, the red rocks here have formed vertical stone pillars that bear witness to the tortuously slow processes of geological time.

The drive from Colorado Springs to the mountain resort of Vail, is a classic crossing of the continental divide. Vail is no anti-climax; it was built in the 1960s as a skiing destination, in a mix of European Alpine styles and continues to draw the crowds to its slopes. The journey back to Denver is long and, because the roads are so good, it is easy to cover distances that would have taken days or weeks when these mountains were first explored by Europeans.

Less than an hour's drive away from Denver, and standing amid the 'flatirons' rocks 5,430 feet above sea level, Boulder is like no other town in Colorado, or even America. It is said to be the cleverest place in the US – home to a major university, the University of Colorado at Boulder and a clutch of government research centres, such as the National Centre for Atmospheric Research and the National Oceanic and Atmospheric Administration. It also has a decidedly 'alternative' edge, exemplified by Pearl Street, which is bathed in seemingly perpetual sunshine. There are few other places in Colorado – or in the US – where you can watch street performers play practically every instrument imaginable, from the didgeridoo to the classical violin. The stately Boulderado Hotel dates back to 1909 and has retained the atmosphere of pre-Space Age America. Musician Louis Armstrong once stayed here at the height of the jazz era and, even though the stained glass ceiling of the hotel's main hall is a replica of the real thing, the mood is still authentically retro.

Boulder seems to stir mixed emotions among native Coloradans. People outside Boulder refer to it being in a bubble of its own. Those who live there talk half seriously of the 'People's Republic of Boulder' – somewhere that is self-consciously liberal – especially in comparison with more conservative-minded places lower down on the plains.

Questions 1–6

Complete the notes below.

Choose **NO MORE THAN TWO WORDS AND/OR A NUMBER** from the passage for each answer.

Write your answers in boxes 1–6 on your answer sheet.

Colorado		
Place	**Height**	**Notes**
Estes Park	1 .... feet	• entry to National Park

Rocky Mountains National Park
• Alpine tundra
• Sub-alpine
• Montane
	1,500ft–14,000 feet	• attracts as many visitors as the much larger
		  2 ....
		• plants adapted to sun and strong
		  3 ....
		• huckleberry, juniper
		• fragrant 4 ....

5	14,440 feet	
Garden of the Gods		• Ancient rocks have taken the shape of 6 ....

Questions 7–13

Do the following statements agree with the Information given in Reading Passage 1?

In boxes 7–13 on your answer sheet, write

YES	if the statement agrees with the information
NO	if the statement contradicts the information
NOT GIVEN	if there is no information on this

7   Vail still serves the purpose for which it was established.

8   Early European explorers were reluctant to make the journey between Vail and Denver.

9   Boulder is known as a place for academics.

10   The National Centre for Atmospheric Research collaborates on projects with the University of Colorado.

11   The street entertainment in Boulder is typical of cities in Colorado.

12   The Boulderado Hotel retains its original ceiling.

13   Boulder is considered by its inhabitants to be different from other cities in the state.

READING PASSAGE 2

You should spend about 20 minutes on **Questions 14–27**, *which are based on Reading Passage 2 below.*

Edward Hopper

A painter captures an era of transition with light

Edward Hopper is widely acknowledged to have been the most important realist painter of twentieth-century America. However, it has been said that his vision of reality was a selective one, reflecting his own temperament in the empty cityscapes, landscapes and isolated figures he painted. His work demonstrates that realism is not merely a literal or photographic copying of what we see, but an interpretive rendering.

Born in a small town outside New York City, Hopper began drawing at a young age. His parents recognised his talent and encouraged him to go to art school. As a young man Hopper worked as a commercial illustrator, studied art in Europe and worked in an artists' colony, where he met and married Josephine Nivison who became his only female model. Hopper made several trips to France as a young man and it was there that he studied the work of Edgar Degas, an artist known for his paintings of ballet dancers. Some of Hopper's paintings display techniques he learnt while studying Degas. Both artists captured fleeting moments when people were absorbed in activities.

During his 84 years, Edward Hopper witnessed dramatic changes in the American way of life. He lived through the Great Depression and the period of economic prosperity that followed. He watched as new technology transformed daily life. In his paintings, Hopper created a visual record of the everyday in the changing country. There is something strangely familiar in his work, as if the viewer had been there to witness each scene. But on closer observation, there is something unsettling about his paintings. Hopper partly achieved this tense quality through his representation of light. Whether exploring the isolation of life in the city or the quiet countryside, Hopper used light to reflect his vision of American life.

The people who inhabit Hopper's paintings often appear to be lost in thought. Hopper rarely discussed the symbolism in his paintings. But today, many art historians believe that, intentionally or not, his paintings are deeply emotional portraits of individuals in society. His interiors especially, with their artificial light and strategic compositions, seem to emphasise his subjects' inner lives.

Hopper said that art should be 'fact seen through a personality' and the mood in the artist's work reflects his introverted quiet disposition. In his 1942 painting *Nighthawks*, Hopper reminds viewers that, even in a crowded city, where you are never totally alone, you might feel lonely. The artificial light in the interior of the diner (restaurant) creates an inviting glow, contrasting with the dark, deserted street. The figures in the painting do not interact with one another. 'Unconsciously,' Hopper said, 'probably I was painting the loneliness of the large city.'

Hopper once said, 'There is a sort of elation about sunlight on the upper part of a house.' The way light hits a building, the forms and shadows it creates, is the key to his artistic style. Hopper developed his compositions like puzzles, trying out the pieces until they made sense. He varied elements in his painting, from the stage in the day to the direction of the light, to set the mood.

The Hoppers bought their first car in 1927 and took many road trips in the years that followed. Hopper also took to the road when looking for inspiration for works like his 1940 work *Gas*. The artist had several real gas stations in mind when he composed this painting and incorporates elements of each to create a composite image. In this painting, Hopper renders both natural and artificial light. The last remnants of sunlight catch on wispy white clouds and electric lights inside the building cast long shadows across the parking lot and illuminate the man's head. The deepest shadows appear in the background where the road disappears into the dark trees. The road is painted on a diagonal line, moving the viewer's eye through the scene, past the gas station and into the unknown down the road.

In 1933, Hopper and his wife, Jo, bought a property on Cape Cod, a popular vacation destination on the coast of Massachusetts in the US. They spent almost every summer there. The artist preferred to spend time in the country, away from the noise, crowds and other distractions of modern city life. In his 1939 painting *Cape Cod Evening*, Hopper divides the scene into simple geometric shapes. He fills the lower half of the

composition with grasses which he observed just outside his studio window. He juxtaposes the grasses, painted with soft earth tones, with the cool blue trees, rendered in a square. Golden light shines on the grasses and house but the trees seem foreboding. The use of colour and light creates a feeling of unease, like the calm before a storm.

Hopper's work has continued to inspire countless artists. In particular, many have reimagined *Nighthawks*, his most famous painting. Film director Alfred Hitchcock based the creepy house in his 1960 thriller *Psycho* on Hopper's painting *House by the Railroad*. Today Hopper is considered one of the most important artists in American history.

Questions 14–20

Answer the questions below.

*Choose **NO MORE THAN THREE WORDS** from the passage for each answer.*

Write your answers in boxes 14–20 on your answer sheet.

14 In what style of art did Edward Hopper paint?

15 Where did Hopper's parents send him when he was young?

16 Where did Hopper meet his wife?

17 What did Hopper see that changed everyday life?

18 What does Hopper use to achieve a sense of tension in his paintings?

19 What aspect of his painting did Hopper seldom talk about?

20 What do many art historians think that Hopper's paintings represented?

Questions 21–25

*Complete each sentence with the correct ending, **A–G**, below.*

*Write the correct answer, **A–G**, in boxes 21–25 on your answer sheet.*

21   Hopper's paintings of scenes indoors

22   In his well-known painting *Nighthawks* Hopper

23   In *Gas*, a painting inspired by a road trip, Hopper

24   Hopper's painting *Cape Cod Evening*

25   More than any of Hopper's other paintings, *Nighthawks* has

A	showed something he could see from where he was working.
B	influenced artists working in various media.
C	established a contrast between the light inside and the lack of light outside.
D	used ideas from a combination of sources to achieve the final result.
E	gave the impression of optimism about the future.
F	conveyed a sense of what the people in his paintings are thinking about.
G	tried to show a new way of looking at the American landscape.

Questions 26 and 27

*Choose **TWO** letters, **A–E**.*

Write the correct letter in boxes 26 and 27 on your answer sheet.

How did Hopper develop his compositions?

A   He produced detailed sketches as a starting point.

B   He experimented with different ideas until the painting fitted together.

C   He used shade on the most important parts of the painting.

D   He altered the point in time at which the scene took place.

E   He kept a travel journal for ideas for paintings.

THINK IT THROUGH

Short answer questions come in the same order as they do in the passage. When you have found some of the answers in the passage, underline them and this will help you locate any that you may have trouble finding.

READING PASSAGE 3

*You should spend about 20 minutes on **Questions 28–40**, which are based on Reading Passage 3 below.*

Animal Extinction

The greatest threat to mankind

A Scientists recognise that species continually disappear at a background extinction rate estimated at about one species per million per year, with new species replacing the lost in a sustainable fashion. From what we understand so far, five great extinction events have reshaped earth in cataclysmic ways in the past 439 million years, each one wiping out between 50 and 95 per cent of the life of the day, including the dominant life forms. New species emerged, but an analysis shows that it takes 10 million years before biological diversity begins to approach what existed before an extinction.

B Today we're living through the sixth great extinction, sometimes known as the Holocene event. This began 50,000 years ago as humans migrated beyond Africa with Stone Age blades, darts and harpoons, entering pristine Ice Age ecosystems and changing them forever by wiping out at least some of the unique megafauna of the times, including the sabre-toothed cats and woolly mammoths. As harmful as our forebears may have been, nothing compares to what is occurring today. Throughout the 20th century the causes of extinction – habitat degradation, overexploitation, agricultural monocultures, human-borne invasive species, human-induced climate-change – increased exponentially.

Most of us think of extinction as the plight of the rhino, tiger, panda or blue whale. But these sagas are only small pieces of the extinction puzzle. Of the 40,168 species that the 10,000 scientists in the World Conservation Union have assessed, one in four mammals, one in eight birds, one in three amphibians, one in three conifers and other gymnosperms are at risk of extinction. By the most conservative measure – based on the last century's recorded extinctions – the current rate of extinction is 100 times the background rate. But Harvard biologist Edward O Wilson estimates that the true rate is more like 1,000 to 10,000 times the background rate.

C A poll by the American Museum of Natural History found that seven in 10 biologists believe that mass extinction poses a colossal threat to human existence and that the dangers of mass extinction are woefully underestimated by almost everyone outside science. In the 200 years since French naturalist Georges Cuvier first floated the concept of extinction, after examining fossil bones and finding 'the existence of a world previous to ours, destroyed by some sort of catastrophe', we have only slowly attempted to correct our own catastrophic behaviour.

D There are a few heartening examples of so-called Lazarus species lost and then found: the Wollemi Pine and the Mahogany Glider in Australia, the Jerdon's Courser in India, the Takahe in New Zealand and the Ivory-billed Woodpecker in the United States have all made a comeback. But virtually all other 'lost' species work their way down the listings from secure to vulnerable, to endangered, to critically endangered, to extinct.

E   Biodiversity is the sum of an area's genes, species and ecosystems (amalgamations of species in their geological and chemical landscapes). The richer an area's biodiversity, the tougher its immune system, since biodiversity includes not only the number of species but also the number of individuals within that species.

Yet it's a mistake to think that critical biodiverse genetic pools exist only in the gaudy show of the coral reefs or the rainforest. Although a hallmark of the desert is sparseness, this is only an illusion. Turn the desert inside out and you'll discover life goes underground in a tangled exuberance of roots and burrows reminiscent of a rainforest canopy, but competing for moisture instead of light. Coyotes dig and maintain wells, probing deep for water. White-winged doves drink enough when the opportunity arises to increase their bodyweight by more than 15 per cent. Black-tailed jack rabbits tolerate internal temperatures of 111°F.

F   Losing even one species irrevocably changes the desert as we know it. Nowhere is this better proven than in a study conducted in the Chihuahuan desert by James H Brown and Edward Heske of the University of New Mexico. When a kangaroo-rat group of species was removed, shrublands quickly converted to grasslands, which supported fewer annual plants, which in turn supported fewer birds. Extinctions lead to co-extinctions because most living things on Earth have a few dependent species, while keystone species influence and support myriad plants and animals.

In a 2004 analysis, Lian Pin Koh predicts that an initially modest co-extinction rate will climb alarmingly as host extinctions rise. Graphed out, the forecast mirrors the rising curve of an infectious epidemic, with the human species acting all the parts: the germ or cause of the problem, the vector or way it is transmitted, and, ultimately, one of up to 100 million victims.

G   Many biologists believe rewilding (restoring land to its natural uncultivated and reintroducing species of wild animal that have been driven out) is the best hope for arresting the sixth great extinction. What we've done until now – protecting pretty landscapes, attempts at sustainable development, community-based conservation and ecosystem management – will not preserve biodiversity through the critical next century. By then, half of all species will be lost, by Wilson's calculation. Only 'megapreserves' large conservation areas – modelled on a deep scientific understanding of what the ecosystem needs will be effective. More than 150 years ago Henry David Thoreau wrote. 'In wildness is the preservation of the world'. This, science finally understands.

Questions 28–35

Reading Passage 3 has seven sections, **A–F**.

Which section contains the following information?

*Write the correct letter, **A–F**, in boxes 28–35 on your answer sheet.*

NB   *You may use any letter more than once.*

28   a reference to a correlation between human activity and extinction

29   examples of survival in a place that is not thought of as an animal habitat

30   an argument that many different species may rely on a single species.

31   examples of species that were endangered and have since increased in numbers

32   details of periods of extinctions before the one Earth is currently experiencing

33   a mention of scientists' opinion of public perception

34   a reference to a possible solution to the loss of species

35   a comparison between species loss and a rapidly spreading disease

THINK IT THROUGH

Matching information

Read the instructions for this kind of task carefully. Not every section from the text will be used. If any sections can be used more than once, this will be included in the instructions.

Questions 36–40

Look at the following statements (Questions 36–40) and the list of researchers below.

Match each statement with the correct researcher, **A–E**.

Write the correct letter, **A–E**, in boxes 36–40 on your answer sheet.

36   The loss of a certain animal had an impact on plants and other animals.

37   The increase in extinction is much greater than what has been reported.

38   Extinction of dependent species will begin slowly and then accelerate.

39   Untamed areas are the key to saving the planet.

40   Evidence showed what was present in the world before a large-scale disaster.

List of Researchers

A   Edward O Wilson

B   Georges Cuvier

C   James H Brown and Edward Heske

D   Lian Pin Koh

E   Henry David Thoreau

WRITING

TASK 1

You should spend about 20 minutes on this task.

> *The diagram below shows the process that is used to treat fresh tea leaves and produce tea bags.*
>
> *Summarise the information by selecting and reporting the main features, and make comparisons where relevant.*

Write at least 150 words.

Manufacture of a tea bag

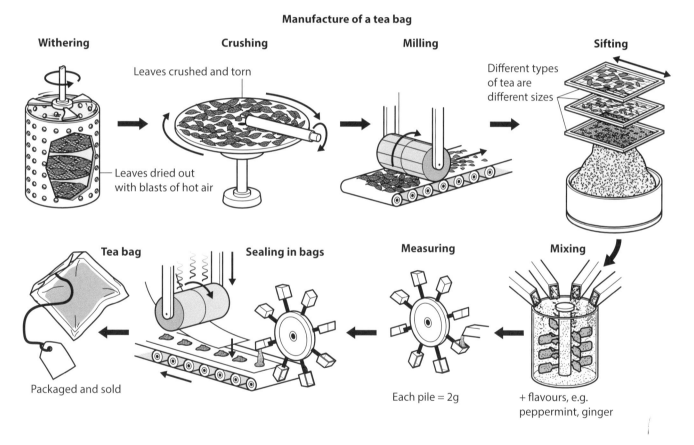

TASK 2

You should spend about 40 minutes on this task.

Write about the following topic:

> *Some people think that a high tax on unhealthy food is the best way to improve people's eating habits. Others think that this is not an effective solution.*
>
> *What is your view?*

Give reasons for your answer and include any relevant examples from your own knowledge or experience.

Write at least 250 words.

SPEAKING

PART 1: Introduction and interview

Weather

- What is your favourite type of weather? Why?

- What is the weather usually like in your country?

- What kind of activities do you enjoy doing in good weather? Why?

- Does the weather affect the way that you feel? Why? / Why not?

Boost your score!

🎧3 10 – 🎧3 12 Listen to Stefan's Speaking test. Make a note of all the different ideas he mentions. How many of his ideas are similar to the ones you talked about? Look at the transcripts on pages 131 and 132. Underline any useful phrases that you could include in your answers.

PART 2: Individual long turn

You will have to talk about the topic for one to two minutes.

You have one minute to think about what you are going to say.

You can make some notes to help you if you wish.

> Talk about a possession (something that you own) that is important to you.
>
> You should say
>
> > what the item is
> >
> > where you got it
> >
> > how long you have had it
>
> and say why it is important to you.

Final question

Are your possessions important to you in general?

PART 3: Two-way discussion

Having a lot of possessions

Does owning a lot of possessions make people happy? Why? / Why not?

Is owning a lot of possessions more important to people nowadays than it was in the past? Why? / Why not?

Shopping and consumerism

What influences people to buy certain products (e.g. advertising, celebrities)? Why?

What are the advantages and disadvantages of a consumer culture for society? Why?

Should the government be responsible for regulating competition among companies in a consumer culture?

IELTS™

SPEAKING: Band Descriptors (public version)

Band	Fluency and coherence	Lexical resource	Grammatical range and accuracy	Pronunciation
9	• speaks fluently with only rare repetition or self-correction; any hesitation is content-related rather than to find words or grammar • speaks coherently with fully appropriate cohesive features • develops topics fully and appropriately	• uses vocabulary with full flexibility and precision in all topics • uses idiomatic language naturally and accurately	• uses a full range of structures naturally and appropriately • produces consistently accurate structures apart from 'slips' characteristic of native speaker speech	• uses a full range of pronunciation features with precision and subtlety • sustains flexible use of features throughout • is effortless to understand
8	• speaks fluently with only occasional repetition or self-correction; hesitation is usually content-related and only rarely to search for language • develops topics coherently and appropriately	• uses a wide vocabulary resource readily and flexibly to convey precise meaning • uses less common and idiomatic vocabulary skilfully, with occasional inaccuracies • uses paraphrase effectively as required	• uses a wide range of structures flexibly • produces a majority of error-free sentences with only very occasional inappropriacies or basic/non-systematic errors	• uses a wide range of pronunciation features • sustains flexible use of features, with only occasional lapses • is easy to understand throughout; L1 accent has minimal effect on intelligibility
7	• speaks at length without noticeable effort or loss of coherence • may demonstrate language-related hesitation at times, or some repetition and/or self-correction • uses a range of connectives and discourse markers with some flexibility	• uses vocabulary resource flexibly to discuss a variety of topics • uses some less common and idiomatic vocabulary and shows some awareness of style and collocation, with some inappropriate choices • uses paraphrase effectively	• uses a range of complex structures with some flexibility • frequently produces error-free sentences, though some grammatical mistakes persist	• shows all the positive features of Band 6 and some, but not all, of the positive features of Band 8
6	• is willing to speak at length, though may lose coherence at times due to occasional repetition, self-correction or hesitation • uses a range of connectives and discourse markers but not always appropriately	• has a wide enough vocabulary to discuss topics at length and make meaning clear in spite of inappropriacies • generally paraphrases successfully	• uses a mix of simple and complex structures, but with limited flexibility • may make frequent mistakes with complex structures though these rarely cause comprehension problems	• uses a range of pronunciation features with mixed control • shows some effective use of features but this is not sustained • can generally be understood throughout, though mispronunciation of individual words or sounds reduces clarity at times
5	• usually maintains flow of speech but uses repetition, self-correction and/or slow speech to keep going • may over-use certain connectives and discourse markers • produces simple speech fluently, but more complex communication causes fluency problems	• manages to talk about familiar and unfamiliar topics but uses vocabulary with limited flexibility • attempts to use paraphrase but with mixed success	• produces basic sentence forms with reasonable accuracy • uses a limited range of more complex structures, but these usually contain errors and may cause some comprehension problems	• shows all the positive features of Band 4 and some, but not all, of the positive features of Band 6
4	• cannot respond without noticeable pauses and may speak slowly, with frequent repetition and self-correction • links basic sentences but with repetitious use of simple connectives and some breakdowns in coherence	• is able to talk about familiar topics but can only convey basic meaning on unfamiliar topics and makes frequent errors in word choice • rarely attempts paraphrase	• produces basic sentence forms and some correct simple sentences but subordinate structures are rare • errors are frequent and may lead to misunderstanding	• uses a limited range of pronunciation features • attempts to control features but lapses are frequent • mispronunciations are frequent and cause some difficulty for the listener
3	• speaks with long pauses • has limited ability to link simple sentences • gives only simple responses and is frequently unable to convey basic message	• uses simple vocabulary to convey personal information • has insufficient vocabulary for less familiar topics	• attempts basic sentence forms but with limited success, or relies on apparently memorised utterances • makes numerous errors except in memorised expressions	• shows some of the features of Band 2 and some, but not all, of the positive features of Band 4
2	• pauses lengthily before most words • little communication possible	• only produces isolated words or memorised utterances	• cannot produce basic sentence forms	• Speech is often unintelligible
1	• no communication possible • no rateable language			
0	• does not attend			

IELTS is jointly owned by the British Council, IDP: IELTS Australia and Cambridge English Language Assessment.

WRITING TASK 1 ASSESSMENT CRITERIA

WRITING TASK 1: Band Descriptors (public version)

Band	Task achievement	Coherence and cohesion	Lexical resource	Grammatical range and accuracy
9	• fully satisfies all the requirements of the task • clearly presents a fully developed response	• uses cohesion in such a way that it attracts no attention • skilfully manages paragraphing	• uses a wide range of vocabulary with very natural and sophisticated control of lexical features; rare minor errors occur only as 'slips'	• uses a wide range of structures with full flexibility and accuracy; rare minor errors occur only as 'slips'
8	• covers all requirements of the task sufficiently • presents, highlights and illustrates key features/ bullet points clearly and appropriately	• sequences information and ideas logically • manages all aspects of cohesion well • uses paragraphing sufficiently and appropriately	• uses a wide range of vocabulary fluently and flexibly to convey precise meanings • skilfully uses uncommon lexical items but there may be occasional inaccuracies in word choice and collocation • produces rare errors in spelling and/or word formation	• uses a wide range of structures • the majority of sentences are error-free • makes only very occasional errors or inappropriacies
7	• covers the requirements of the task • (A) presents a clear overview of main trends, differences or stages • (GT) presents a clear purpose, with the tone consistent and appropriate • clearly presents and highlights key features/bullet points but could be more fully extended	• logically organises information and ideas; there is clear progression throughout • uses a range of cohesive devices appropriately although there may be some under-/over-use	• uses a sufficient range of vocabulary to allow some flexibility and precision • uses less common lexical items with some awareness of style and collocation • may produce occasional errors in word choice, spelling and/or word formation	• uses a variety of complex structures • produces frequent error-free sentences • has good control of grammar and punctuation but may make a few errors
6	• addresses the requirements of the task • (A) presents an overview with information appropriately selected • (GT) presents a purpose that is generally clear; there may be inconsistencies in tone • presents and adequately highlights key features/ bullet points but details may be irrelevant, inappropriate or inaccurate	• arranges information and ideas coherently and there is a clear overall progression • uses cohesive devices effectively, but cohesion within and/or between sentences may be faulty or mechanical • may not always use referencing clearly or appropriately	• uses an adequate range of vocabulary for the task • attempts to use less common vocabulary but with some inaccuracy • makes some errors in spelling and/or word formation, but they do not impede communication	• uses a mix of simple and complex sentence forms • makes some errors in grammar and punctuation but they rarely reduce communication
5	• generally addresses the task; the format may be inappropriate in places • (A) recounts detail mechanically with no clear overview; there may be no data to support the description • (GT) may present a purpose for the letter that is unclear at times; the tone may be variable and sometimes inappropriate • presents, but inadequately covers, key features/ bullet points; there may be a tendency to focus on details	• presents information with some organisation but there may be a lack of overall progression • makes inadequate, inaccurate or over-use of cohesive devices • may be repetitive because of lack of referencing and substitution	• uses a limited range of vocabulary, but this is minimally adequate for the task • may make noticeable errors in spelling and/or word formation that may cause some difficulty for the reader	• uses only a limited range of structures • attempts complex sentences but these tend to be less accurate than simple sentences • may make frequent grammatical errors and punctuation may be faulty; errors can cause some difficulty for the reader
4	• attempts to address the task but does not cover all key features/bullet points; the format may be inappropriate • (GT) fails to clearly explain the purpose of the letter; the tone may be inappropriate • may confuse key features/bullet points with detail; parts may be unclear, irrelevant, repetitive or inaccurate	• presents information and ideas but these are not arranged coherently and there is no clear progression in the response • uses some basic cohesive devices but these may be inaccurate or repetitive	• uses only basic vocabulary which may be used repetitively or which may be inappropriate for the task • has limited control of word formation and/or spelling; • errors may cause strain for the reader	• uses only a very limited range of structures with only rare use of subordinate clauses • some structures are accurate but errors predominate, and punctuation is often faulty
3	• fails to address the task, which may have been completely misunderstood • presents limited ideas which may be largely irrelevant/repetitive	• does not organise ideas logically • may use a very limited range of cohesive devices, and those used may not indicate a logical relationship between ideas	• uses only a very limited range of words and expressions with very limited control of word formation and/or spelling • errors may severely distort the message	• attempts sentence forms but errors in grammar and punctuation predominate and distort the meaning
2	• answer is barely related to the task	• has very little control of organisational features	• uses an extremely limited range of vocabulary; essentially no control of word formation and/or spelling	• cannot use sentence forms except in memorised phrases
1	• answer is completely unrelated to the task	• fails to communicate any message	• can only use a few isolated words	• cannot use sentence forms at all
0	• does not attend • does not attempt the task in any way • writes a totally memorised response			

(A) Academic I (GT) General Training

PHOTOCOPIABLE

IELTS

WRITING TASK 2: Band Descriptors (public version)

Band	Task response	Coherence and cohesion	Lexical resource	Grammatical range and accuracy
9	• fully addresses all parts of the task • presents a fully developed position in answer to the question with relevant, fully extended and well supported ideas	• uses cohesion in such a way that it attracts no attention • skilfully manages paragraphing	• uses a wide range of vocabulary with very natural and sophisticated control of lexical features; rare minor errors occur only as 'slips'	• uses a wide range of structures with full flexibility and accuracy; rare minor errors occur only as 'slips'
8	• sufficiently addresses all parts of the task • presents a well-developed response to the question with relevant, extended and supported ideas	• sequences information and ideas logically • manages all aspects of cohesion well • uses paragraphing sufficiently and appropriately	• uses a wide range of vocabulary fluently and flexibly to convey precise meanings • skilfully uses uncommon lexical items but there may be occasional inaccuracies in word choice and collocation • produces rare errors in spelling and/or word formation	• uses a wide range of structures • the majority of sentences are error-free • makes only very occasional errors or inappropriacies
7	• addresses all parts of the task • presents a clear position throughout the response • presents, extends and supports main ideas, but there may be a tendency to over-generalise and/or supporting ideas may lack focus	• logically organises information and ideas; there is clear progression throughout • uses a range of cohesive devices appropriately although there may be some under-/over-use • presents a clear central topic within each paragraph	• uses a sufficient range of vocabulary to allow some flexibility and precision • uses less common lexical items with some awareness of style and collocation • may produce occasional errors in word choice, spelling and/or word formation	• uses a variety of complex structures • produces frequent error-free sentences • has good control of grammar and punctuation but may make a few errors
6	• addresses all parts of the task although some parts may be more fully covered than others • presents a relevant position although the conclusions may become unclear or repetitive • presents relevant main ideas but some may be inadequately developed/unclear	• arranges information and ideas coherently and there is a clear overall progression • uses cohesive devices effectively, but cohesion within and/or between sentences may be faulty or mechanical • may not always use referencing clearly or appropriately • uses paragraphing, but not always logically	• uses an adequate range of vocabulary for the task • attempts to use less common vocabulary but with some inaccuracy • makes some errors in spelling and/or word formation, but they do not impede communication	• uses a mix of simple and complex sentence forms • makes some errors in grammar and punctuation but they rarely reduce communication
5	• addresses the task only partially; the format may be inappropriate in places • expresses a position but the development is not always clear and there may be no conclusions drawn • presents some main ideas but these are limited and not sufficiently developed; there may be irrelevant detail	• presents information with some organisation but there may be a lack of overall progression • makes inadequate, inaccurate or over-use of cohesive devices • may be repetitive because of lack of referencing and substitution • may not write in paragraphs, or paragraphing may be inadequate	• uses a limited range of vocabulary, but this is minimally adequate for the task • may make noticeable errors in spelling and/or word formation that may cause some difficulty for the reader	• uses only a limited range of structures • attempts complex sentences but these tend to be less accurate than simple sentences • may make frequent grammatical errors and punctuation may be faulty; errors can cause some difficulty for the reader
4	• responds to the task only in a minimal way or the answer is tangential; the format may be inappropriate • presents a position but this is unclear • presents some main ideas but these are difficult to identify and may be repetitive, irrelevant or not well supported	• presents information and ideas but these are not arranged coherently and there is no clear progression in the response • uses some basic cohesive devices but these may be inaccurate or repetitive • may not write in paragraphs or their use may be confusing	• uses only basic vocabulary which may be used repetitively or which may be inappropriate for the task • has limited control of word formation and/or spelling; errors may cause strain for the reader	• uses only a very limited range of structures with only rare use of subordinate clauses • some structures are accurate but errors predominate, and punctuation is often faulty
3	• does not adequately address any part of the task • does not express a clear position • presents few ideas, which are largely undeveloped or irrelevant	• does not organise ideas logically • may use a very limited range of cohesive devices, and those used may not indicate a logical relationship between ideas	• uses only a very limited range of words and expressions with very limited control of word formation and/or spelling • errors may severely distort the message	• attempts sentence forms but errors in grammar and punctuation predominate and distort the meaning
2	• barely responds to the task • does not express a position • may attempt to present one or two ideas but there is no development	• has very little control of organisational features	• uses an extremely limited range of vocabulary; essentially no control of word formation and/or spelling	• cannot use sentence forms except in memorised phrases
1	• answer is completely unrelated to the task	• fails to communicate any message	• can only use a few isolated words	• cannot use sentence forms at all
0	• does not attend • does not attempt the task in any way • writes a totally memorised response			

Reproduced with permission of Cambridge English Language Assessment ©UCLES 2017

IELTS is jointly owned by the British Council, IDP: IELTS Australia and the University of Cambridge ESOL Examinations (Cambridge ESOL).

BRITISH COUNCIL

idp
IELTS AUSTRALIA

CAMBRIDGE ENGLISH
Language Assessment
Part of the University of Cambridge

IELTS Listening and Reading Answer Sheet

Centre number:

Pencil must be used to complete this sheet.

Please write your **full name** in CAPITAL letters on the line below:

_____

Then write your six digit Candidate number in the boxes and shade the number in the grid on the right.

0 1 2 3 4 5 6 7 8 9
0 1 2 3 4 5 6 7 8 9
0 1 2 3 4 5 6 7 8 9
0 1 2 3 4 5 6 7 8 9
0 1 2 3 4 5 6 7 8 9
0 1 2 3 4 5 6 7 8 9

Test date (shade ONE box for the day, ONE box for the month and ONE box for the year):

Day: 01 02 03 04 05 06 07 08 09 10 11 12 13 14 15 16 17 18 19 20 21 22 23 24 25 26 27 28 29 30 31

Month: 01 02 03 04 05 06 07 08 09 10 11 12   **Year** (last 2 digits): 13 14 15 16 17 18 19 20 21

Listening   Listening   Listening   Listening   Listening   Listening

#	Answer	Marker use only	#	Answer	Marker use only
1		✓ 1 ✗	21		✓ 21 ✗
2		✓ 2 ✗	22		✓ 22 ✗
3		✓ 3 ✗	23		✓ 23 ✗
4		✓ 4 ✗	24		✓ 24 ✗
5		✓ 5 ✗	25		✓ 25 ✗
6		✓ 6 ✗	26		✓ 26 ✗
7		✓ 7 ✗	27		✓ 27 ✗
8		✓ 8 ✗	28		✓ 28 ✗
9		✓ 9 ✗	29		✓ 29 ✗
10		✓ 10 ✗	30		✓ 30 ✗
11		✓ 11 ✗	31		✓ 31 ✗
12		✓ 12 ✗	32		✓ 32 ✗
13		✓ 13 ✗	33		✓ 33 ✗
14		✓ 14 ✗	34		✓ 34 ✗
15		✓ 15 ✗	35		✓ 35 ✗
16		✓ 16 ✗	36		✓ 36 ✗
17		✓ 17 ✗	37		✓ 37 ✗
18		✓ 18 ✗	38		✓ 38 ✗
19		✓ 19 ✗	39		✓ 39 ✗
20		✓ 20 ✗	40		✓ 40 ✗

Marker 2 Signature

Marker 1 Signature

Listening Total

IELTS L-R v1.0

denote Print Limited 0121 520 5100

DP787/394

Reproduced with permission of Cambridge English Language Assessment ©UCLES 2017

Please write your **full name** in CAPITAL letters on the line below:

_____

Please write your Candidate number on the line below:

_____

Please write your three digit language code in the boxes and shade the numbers in the grid on the right.

Are you: Female? ▭   Male? ▭

Reading   Reading   Reading   Reading   Reading   Reading

Module taken (shade one box):   Academic ▭   General Training ▭

	Marker use only			Marker use only
1	✓ 1 ✗	21		✓ 21 ✗
2	✓ 2 ✗	22		✓ 22 ✗
3	✓ 3 ✗	23		✓ 23 ✗
4	✓ 4 ✗	24		✓ 24 ✗
5	✓ 5 ✗	25		✓ 25 ✗
6	✓ 6 ✗	26		✓ 26 ✗
7	✓ 7 ✗	27		✓ 27 ✗
8	✓ 8 ✗	28		✓ 28 ✗
9	✓ 9 ✗	29		✓ 29 ✗
10	✓ 10 ✗	30		✓ 30 ✗
11	✓ 11 ✗	31		✓ 31 ✗
12	✓ 12 ✗	32		✓ 32 ✗
13	✓ 13 ✗	33		✓ 33 ✗
14	✓ 14 ✗	34		✓ 34 ✗
15	✓ 15 ✗	35		✓ 35 ✗
16	✓ 16 ✗	36		✓ 36 ✗
17	✓ 17 ✗	37		✓ 37 ✗
18	✓ 18 ✗	38		✓ 38 ✗
19	✓ 19 ✗	39		✓ 39 ✗
20	✓ 20 ✗	40		✓ 40 ✗

Marker 2 Signature		Marker 1 Signature		Reading Total	

Transcripts

Boost Your Score

Listening (pages 6–7)

 Exercise 2b

a) …Professor Shaw has now had several books published under her name alone, but in fact her first published work was written in collaboration with a well-known historian, who has appeared on several television programmes.

b) For those of you who haven't been to the College before, you'll need to know about its location. In fact, it's easy to find, on the west side of the town, not far from the river, and about a mile from the town centre.

c) …there are numerous artworks in the museum that will be familiar to members of the public, but one that particularly stands out is entirely assembled from glass. This rather eye-catching piece is surrounded by various stone and wood sculptures.

d) Educational technology has recently been introduced, and one of its chief benefits has been to increase the amount of time students have in which to complete their assignments.

e) Your tutors recommended a number of areas of research for this project, but it seems that many of you were unable to get hold of the journal we mentioned, which would have been of much greater relevance than the library books and, in some cases websites, that you used.

f) All assignments must be completed by the end of term, but before you embark on your essay, we strongly advise you to hand in a proposal including all your main arguments and evidence. This is for your own benefit and to help with your planning and time management.

 Exercise 3a

Anish Kapoor is a contemporary artist whose sculptures are installed in public spaces all over the world. In fact, many of his works have become landmarks in the communities where they are located, and are particularly striking due to their size. Because his works are so enormous, they are described as interacting with and changing the space around them.

Although he currently lives and works in London, Kapoor was actually born in India, in 1954, and that's where he spent his childhood. After moving to Israel for a couple of years, he eventually relocated to England in the seventies to attend Art School, and has been based in the UK since then.

Nowadays, several of his sculptures are tourist attractions and popular with locals too. In Chicago, visitors can walk around and underneath one artwork in a public park known as *The Bean*. The surface of the sculpture is reflective, and encourages people to look at themselves and the surrounding architecture of the city in new and unexpected ways.

Another popular piece was built by Kapoor in 2009 specifically to fit snugly into the New Zealand landscape. It sits on a grassy hillside, and from the outside, could be said to resemble a giant trumpet. The work is almost the length of a football field, and has an interior space, so it is impossible to view all at once, and in order to fully understand its shape, members of the public must move around the piece and look through it.

Kapoor constructed the bright red sculpture using a combination of materials, chiefly a special type of flexible plastic for the main body of the work, and with supports made from steel. Despite these industrial materials, the piece is said to have a natural, organic quality.

In 2012, the Olympic games were held in London, and Kapoor was commissioned to build a permanent sculpture to stand in the Olympic Park. Working in collaboration with Cecil Balmond, an innovative and contemporary engineer, he produced *Orbit*, a winding, asymmetrical tower which blurs the line between art and architecture. With works such as this, Kapoor continues to push the boundaries of what art can be.

After parts of Japan were devastated by natural disaster in 2011, Kapoor was moved to make art by way of a response, and developed a piece entitled *Ark Nova*. The inflatable structure is a venue for performance, with an interior that can hold 500 people. Kapoor's vision was to create a space that could travel, and uniquely, the deflated venue can be moved to a new location after each performance.

Visitors to art galleries and museums, and even those casually passing his public works develop a physical relationship with Kapoor's work, and one of the main characteristics of Kapoor's art is the principle that the viewer's interaction with his art is as important as the art itself. In this way, his work helps people experience space differently.

Boost Your Score

Speaking (pages 14–15)

 Exercise 1

a) What do you like about the place where you live?
I love the place where I live because I have a garden and my flat is near the shops.

b) How often do you go shopping?
I go to the supermarket about three times a week.

c) What was the last book that you read?
I can't remember.

 Exercise 2b

a) What do you like about the place where you live?
I live in a small flat which I like because it's very modern and I really like the way it is decorated, especially the kitchen which is quite big. I share my flat with two friends, and we get on very well together. It's also in a really nice area, near the shops, although I would prefer it if we were a bit closer to the train station or a bus stop.

b) How often do you go shopping?
I go to the supermarket about three times a week because I need to buy food, but I don't really enjoy doing the food shopping. I love going to buy clothes though, and I suppose I go shopping for clothes about once a month. I prefer to go alone so that I can take my time trying things on.

c) What was the last book that you read?
Actually I can't remember the last book I read, but it was probably a novel, because that's what I usually read. I love reading but I don't have as much time to read as I would like to. Reading books and magazines in English is difficult but it helps me increase my vocabulary.

 ### Exercise 2d

What was the last book that you read?
M: Oh, I don't really enjoy reading that much, I prefer watching TV. I love all kinds of programmes including soaps, documentaries, news programmes… I probably watch about two hours a day. The last programme I watched was a comedy – it was really funny and I'd recommend it.

 ### Exercise 4b

M: How important is it for children to do sports at school?
F: I think it is essential for children to do sports for many reasons. Firstly, doing sports is good exercise and will have a positive effect on children's health. It is important for their fitness. I also think it is good for children to learn to work together with others, which is something they can learn in team sports like football or basketball. Another advantage is that going outside and getting some exercise will help children to concentrate when they go back to the classroom.
M: Do you think it is good for children to play competitive sports and games?
F: Well, in my opinion, learning about competition at school is useful in some ways. For example, it can prepare children for the real world, and maybe it could teach them to try their best. On the other hand, for very small children, perhaps they should have the chance to play sports without focusing on winning, so they learn to enjoy sports and games without too much pressure.

Practice Test 1

Listening (page 16)

 ### Section 1

You will hear a conversation between a woman who wants information about a language school and the school administrator.

First, you have some time to look at questions one to five.

(Pause)

You will see that there is an example that has been done for you. On this occasion only, the conversation relating to this will be played first.

M: Good morning, this is The Bridge Language School, can I help you?
F: Yes, I'd like some information about courses, please.
M: OK, well, I'm the school administrator and my name is Steven. What would you like to know?

The school administrator is called Steven, so Steven has been written in the space. Now we shall begin. You should answer the questions as you listen because you will not hear the recording a second time.

Listen carefully and answer questions one to five.

M: Good morning, this is The Bridge Language School can I help you?
F: Yes, I'd like some information about courses, please.
M: OK, well, I'm the school administrator and my name is Steven. What would you like to know?
F: When is your next language course? My neighbour wants to join an English class. He's a beginner.
M: Mmm… well… there is a course running now, but it finishes in July, and then the next will start in September. That one runs until December.
F: That's great. And are there classes every day?
M: No, in fact the language lessons take place in the mornings on a Tuesday and Friday every week.
F: Perfect.
M: Actually we've just got a new teacher who arrived last month. She's very popular with the students. Her name is Mrs Reade.
F: …is that R double E-D?
M: No, R-E-A-D-E. Got that?
F: Thanks.
M: So if your neighbour is a new student, he needs to come in himself to fill in some details before the course starts.
F: That's fine. Does he need to bring his passport in?
M: That won't be necessary, but he does need to have a photo with him so we can make up a student card.
F: No problem. And while I'm here, can you give me any information about your other courses, such as French and Spanish? I'd be interested in coming to one of those myself.
M: Oh good, they are fun classes! But I only deal with English courses, you'll need to call my colleague for more information. She's Susan, and she's on 5-7-3 double 9-2.
F: Thank you.

Before you hear the rest of the conversation, you have some time to look at questions six to ten.

(Pause)

Now listen and answer questions six to ten.

F: I wonder if you could also give me some information about the social activities you organise for students?
M: Of course. We have a really good social programme here, and there is something happening every week. On Wednesday evenings we always have a meal for students in a local restaurant, and on Fridays there's a big party every week in the town centre.
F: That sounds good. And how about trips to other places – do you have any of those?
M: Mmm, there are regular trips to nearby cities and places of interest. In a few weeks we have one to London, for example. Students like coming with us because the trips tend to be really good value – the London one is just forty pounds, which is a great price. It includes the travel costs as well as a tour of the main sights, and the entrance fee to a place where we always take the students, a museum about the history of the city.
F: OK. And are there any other events based here?
M: Yes, I forgot to mention the regular music club, and also the film club. Students enjoy listening to live music in a local hall, while the film club is in a local hotel … oh no, it's changed venues, sorry, it's now at the library.
F: Lovely. So if my neighbour wants to attend any of these events, how should he do that?
M: Well, he needs to sign his name on a list for any event. We have all the up-to-date details about these on a noticeboard in the café, and if he sees anything he fancies, he should add his name to the list in the office.

Practice Test 1

Listening (page 17)

 Section 2

You will hear part of a talk by a holiday resort representative to a group of holidaymakers

First you have some time to look at questions eleven to fifteen.

(Pause)

Listen carefully, and answer questions eleven to fifteen.

Hello everyone and welcome to Morbourne Holiday resort. My name's Tom and I'm one of the resort representatives. I'm here to give you some information about where things are and what events are going on in the next few days.

Now, take a look at the maps you've all been given, as I want to point out one or two things. You can see the hotel where we are now at the bottom of the map, and if you look on the right-hand side of the map, you should see the lake and the play area for children. If you're interested in some relaxing beauty treatments, I can highly recommend the beauty spa, which is located by the entrance to the play area – that's the entrance by the lake, not the one in front of the hotel.

If you're looking for something a bit more active, we have a fitness class which takes place every day outdoors, and that's held in the beautiful gardens near the swimming pool – if you come out of the hotel and walk along the road, past the multi-sports pitches, you'll see the swimming pool on your left, and the gardens are behind that building.

Another great activity to do here is cycling around the area, and the bike hire is always popular with guests. If you're planning to hire bikes for the family, you'll need to head for the far side of the lake and you'll see the bikes there.

I can see we have a lot of families here this week, so please make use of our kids club. There will be staff supervising activities for young children every afternoon until five o'clock. If you've been here before, you'll remember it used to be located by the multi-sports pitches but now there is a brand new building for this on the opposite side of the road just in front of the hotel.

Finally, you have probably already seen the little shop inside the hotel selling newspapers – that's on the ground floor at the right of the entrance, but if you're looking to buy souvenirs, there's a shop for that a few metres down the road – just go past the swimming pool and it's on the left.

Before you hear the rest of the talk, you have some time to look at questions sixteen to twenty.

(Pause)

Now listen and answer questions sixteen to twenty.

Now I'm going to tell you a bit more about the resort so you can get the best from your stay here. As you probably know, we are about six kilometres away from the town centre, so if you're feeling energetic, it's possible to walk there and back. There is also a train that leaves from the station south of here, but if you want to save time, the fastest mode of transport is actually the bus, as it takes a direct route right into the centre.

As for the hotel, well, the restaurant is here on the first floor and all the rooms are upstairs on the second floor. As you can see, the setting is traditional and peaceful, while still having plenty of modern facilities. Every room is fully equipped with air conditioning, and wherever your room is, there is a stunning view – rooms at the front overlook the lake while guests at the back of the hotel can see the pretty village down the hill, and whichever side you're staying on, you can see the mountains surrounding us.

You should have everything you need for a wonderful stay, but if there is anything we can help you with, our staff are always ready to look after your needs. All meals are included, that's breakfast, lunch and an evening meal, and for just a small additional cost we can supply extras such as afternoon tea, it would be our pleasure.

Well, we're looking forward to a really great week of good weather! According to the recent forecast, the temperature next week should reach around thirty-two degrees Celsius – that's just above the average for the moment, which is thirty-one, and a lot warmer than last week when it didn't get any higher than twenty-six degrees.

Bearing the weather in mind, there are a couple of organised activities you might be interested in tomorrow. At about a quarter past ten a group will be meeting in front of the hotel for a hike in the local area led by one of our guides. If you like the sound of that, just come along then. Also tomorrow morning is our first sailing class - anyone who wants to try that should meet at the lake. Bring a swimming costume and get there by ten.

I'm sure you'll enjoy your stay here…

Practice Test 1

Listening (pages 18–19)

 Section 3

You will hear a conversation between an art student called Peter and his tutor.

First, you have some time to look at questions twenty-one to twenty-five.

(Pause)

Listen carefully, and answer questions twenty-one to twenty-five.

M: Hello Dr Wilson, I was hoping to talk to you about the course I want to take next term and ask your advice on one or two things.
F: Yes, certainly. It's the course in Art Conservation that you're thinking of taking isn't it?
M: That's right. I'm very interested in a future career in an art gallery, and one of the other lecturers said this course could be good preparation. Having said that, my sister did a similar course and she loved it, but wasn't convinced it would be right for me.
F: Well, I spoke to one of your classmates last week who thought you'd do well on the course and I have to agree.
M: Oh good.
F: And I understand you've been finding out a bit more about working in art conservation…?

M: Yes, I called one of the restorers from the art museum in the city, and we had a long conversation. I felt quite inspired by what she said about the pleasure of leaving art in good condition for future generations, and it was interesting to hear about the range of artists and others she collaborates with. In her view though, it's the opportunities to expand your knowledge that bring the greatest job satisfaction.

F: Wonderful! So do you think there are any gaps in your skills or knowledge at the moment?

M: Hmm, I'm not entirely sure. I think I could do with revising what I know about the history of art as that's bound to be useful.

F: OK, that is relevant to the course, but I think it's an area that you're already very familiar with. I think you do need to brush up on the scientific aspects of this subject – the use of chemicals and laboratory equipment in art conservation is something you'll need a thorough understanding of. Another requirement is to be efficient and well-organised, but I've seen plenty of evidence of that from you already.

M: Right, thank you.

F: Now you've just done some volunteering in this area I think…?

M: Yes, I worked as a volunteer at the gallery of traditional art alongside a couple of art conservationists. I did two weeks and it was really helpful for me.

F: Good. And was the job everything that you had expected?

M: Most of it was, yes. One thing that struck me actually was the amount of physical work – with the larger sculptures we had to get up ladders and sometimes move very heavy objects around, which I hadn't previously considered would be required, but then there was also a lot of sitting at a desk writing up descriptions of what had been done, which was more what I could have predicted the job would be.

F: And did you learn much about future professional training and development?

M: Yes, but actually I'd read up on that before volunteering so I already knew about that.

F: Good. So you'll have a few weeks before the course starts – have you got any plans for the next month?

M: Actually I was looking forward to visiting the History Museum in the city as they've got a large conservation department there, but I've heard that it's being renovated, so there isn't much point going there at the moment. I'm really excited about getting started on a little task by myself, as I've got a couple of pieces from an antique shop that I think I can practise my restoration skills on.

F: Good idea. And haven't you arranged to get together with a professor of art who specialises in this area, for a chat?

M: Yes, I tried to but he's away at the moment, so I'm hoping to sort that out in a few months' time.

Before you hear the rest of the conversation, you have some time to look at questions twenty-six to thirty.

(Pause)

Now listen, and answer questions twenty-six to thirty.

F: Now, do you want to talk about the introductory workshops on the course? You'll need to decide which ones you'd like to take, but I can tell you a bit more about them first if you like?

M: Yes, thanks. So first on the list is the ceramics workshop – I've heard that it's not at all like the other courses as it's taught quite differently…

F: Well, I wouldn't say that. It actually links theory and practice very closely, so you learn skills that you can use straightaway, but I wouldn't say it was particularly unusual. I'm not sure it's an area that'll suit you, necessarily.

M: OK. And what about the module on cleaning paintings?

F: Well, if you like the sound of that, sign up for it soon because it can be quite difficult to book a place. Based on previous experience, demand from students has been high.

M: Yes, I'd heard that. It's highly recommended.

F: Then there's a workshop on looking after picture frames. The supervisors on that session are both professional frame restorers who've spent years in the field. Well worth going to.

M: Yes, I read their profiles on the website and I think I could learn a lot from them. There are so many good options, though, I'm finding it hard to choose! How would you describe the workshop on sculptures?

F: That's interesting because students are asked to select which type of material to work with, there's a choice of working with wood, metal or stone.

M: That sounds as though it would be good for anyone specialising in those materials, but maybe not for me.

F: I think it has a broad enough focus. And the other one is about how to work with paper.

M: I have had some experience of conserving works of art on paper when I looked at drawings and sketches.

F: Mmm. This workshop can present quite a challenge for the less studious, as it really does require a lot of background reading and research to learn how to work with the paper.

M: I see. Well, thanks very much for all your help, Dr Wilson.

Practice Test 1

Listening (page 20)

 Section 4

You will hear a science student giving a presentation about a young boy who has become a successful inventor.

First you have some time to look at questions thirty-one to forty.

(Pause)

Now listen carefully and answer questions thirty-one to forty.

Good morning everyone. My presentation today is about creativity, invention and an exceptional young boy.

Peyton Robertson is an American teenager who is stunning the world of science with his innovative thinking and his drive to solve problems. He has been highly praised and gained a degree of fame for his practical inventions that aim to make the world a better place. He initially came up with a plan when listening to the news about the effects of a huge hurricane on the East Coast of the USA.

People struggled to hold back the water that surged across the land, and by the time the floods had receded, thousands had been forced to leave the area, and billions of dollars of damage had been caused. One of the biggest issues with seawater flooding is the destruction caused when salt reacts with building materials such as metal and concrete. The extent of the damage can be contained to some degree by fast and thorough cleaning up after the water has drained away. However, if the salt isn't cleaned away effectively, it can corrode buildings, roads and pavements, and cause continuing problems for electrical systems.

According to civil engineers, the best way to stop most flood damage is with preventative measures. The most common of these is the construction of walls to block surges of water in places that are considered to be at risk.

However, in the case of an extreme storm, this may not be sufficient, and that's when emergency crews turn to a last resort – filling sandbags to build temporary barriers. Sandbags are very common as a water barrier, but they have their pros and cons. While they have in their favour being cheap and easy to make, they are also heavy, and manoeuvring them into place can be hard work, even causing injury.

(Pause)

So after listening to the news, twelve-year-old Peyton started thinking – he wanted to come up with something other than sand to fill the bags with. He found that there was already an alternative filling, which was polymer, a type of plastic, – but this was too light to hold back the water. His idea was to add salt. This increased the weight, but reduced the amount the polymer could expand, which in turn stopped it from soaking up the water. Through numerous calculations and a process of trial and error, Peyton eventually settled on the right amount of salt to add to the bags.

Having resolved that challenge, Peyton then developed the bags further by designing and adding fasteners, enabling the bags to be strongly connected in order to form an extremely effective barrier.

With his new design fully formed, Peyton made a video about his invention and entered a competition for young scientists. He was selected as one of several finalists. Peyton was given a further three months to tweak his invention before presenting it to the judges in person, and to this end, was assigned a scientist who could give advice and guidance.

Peyton travelled to Minnesota to meet the judges, and after demonstrating his prototype, he was awarded the top prize, which included twenty-five thousand dollars as well as a trip to Costa Rica.

Not content with this achievement, Peyton is now thinking about his next project, and he has again been inspired by stories in local news reports. In Florida, where he lives, fruit growers are currently suffering as a particular disease causes citrus fruit to drop early, and Peyton is now investigating the possibility of immunising the trees from this disease.

So what is the secret of this young boy's incredible success? Perhaps it's all down to his attitude. It seems that other young inventors and innovators could learn from his example when he says that he is not daunted or discouraged when experiments don't succeed as intended, but rather learns from them. This way of looking at experimental work is surely key to progress and accomplishment.

Practice Test 1

Speaking (page 33)

 Part 1

M: Good afternoon. Can you please tell me your name?
F: My name is Rosa Bertrán.
M: And where do you come from, Rosa?
F: I'm from Spain, but actually I was born in Cuba. I only lived there for a few years though.
M: Thank you. Now in the first part of the test, I'd like to find out a bit about you. Let's talk about sports. Do you enjoy playing any sports? *I had been playing*
F: Well, I used to like swimming and I really love playing tennis, but unfortunately I haven't done much sport recently.
M: Why not?
F: I've just been very busy with my studies, and I haven't had enough free time.
M: So did you do more or less sport when you were a child?
F: Oh, I definitely did more. As I said, I used to swim and in fact I was in a club at school. I swam in competitions, and I trained regularly until I was about seventeen. I also did lots of other sports just for fun, although I wasn't so good at them.
M: Do you think it is important for all children to play sports at school?
F: Absolutely.
M: Why?
F: Because playing a sport can teach many things. Children can learn how important it is to practise and work hard, and if they do team sports, they can learn how to work well with other people too. Of course, it is also good for keeping fit and living a healthy lifestyle, and when people do sports regularly in childhood, then maybe they will be more likely to continue with exercise when they are older. This is probably the most important reason for sports being part of the school timetable – to improve the health of future generations.
M: Are there any sports that you would like to try in the future?
F: Mmm, let me think… perhaps I would like to try a more exciting sport, like sailing or climbing…
M: Why?
F: Because they are not the kind of sports you do at school as a child, and I think they could be fun.

Practice Test 1

Speaking (page 33)

 Part 2

M: In this part of the test, I'm going to give you a topic to talk about. You should talk about the topic for one to two minutes. You have one minute to think about what you are going to say and you can make notes if you want to. I would like you to talk about a time when you were late for something.

(pause)

M: Remember, you should talk for one to two minutes, and I'll tell you when the time is up.

F: OK. I am going to talk about a time when I was late for an important event, and the event I was late for was my brother's birthday party. It was about five years ago, I think, and it was a very important birthday for my brother because he was twenty-five years old, and he decided to celebrate with a very big party. He had invited all his friends and family to a beach, because it was summertime, and there was food and music and swimming at the beach. He told us to be there at eight o'clock in the evening so we could go swimming and dance to music before we ate dinner. I lived in the same town but on the other side of the town, and I had to take a bus to get there. So the bus was stuck in traffic and it took much longer than usual. It was late, and when I got on the bus, we were in a traffic jam. In the end, I got to the party at about nine o'clock. I was later than all my family, so my brother, my parents, my cousins and my brother's friends were all waiting for me. They were all worried about me. I had tried to text them to say I was going to be late, but there was a poor signal, and they didn't see my messages! I felt very bad because I knew my brother wanted me to be there earlier.

M: Thank you. Are you often late for events?

F: No I'm not. Generally speaking, I'm a punctual person and I really don't like to be late for anything.

M: Thank you.

Practice Test 1

Speaking (page 33)

 Part 3

M: Now, let's talk about being on time in general. How important is it to be on time in your country?

F: Well, in Spain we are definitely more relaxed about being on time than in some other countries. I think that there is a stereotype about Spanish people that we are often late for things. But as I said before, I am a punctual person, and actually a lot of my friends and family nowadays try not to be late, so I think maybe it is changing. But it depends – if you are going to a job interview or an important appointment, people expect you to be on time. If you are meeting a friend for coffee, it is not so important.

M: OK, and can you tell me what people can do to make sure they are on time for important events?

F: Yes, that's a difficult question. Let me think… well… one idea is to keep a diary and use it carefully. I usually put important events in my diary, and then I check it regularly to see what I should be doing. Another good idea is to wear a watch, or at least check the time on your phone whenever you have to go somewhere. Oh, and it can be helpful to set an alarm to remind you about events, and give you enough time to get there. It is really important to give yourself enough time to get ready for things, and enough time to travel.

M: Let's move on to talk about politeness. Do you think it is as important to be polite nowadays as it was in the past?

F: Yes, of course. I think that is something that doesn't change. It is always important to be polite. Some older people might think that younger people are less polite today than in the past but in my opinion, that is not true. I firmly believe that politeness is important for all generations.

M: What are some of the things that people can do to show respect for others, apart from being on time?

F: Hmmm… let me think about that … well, I think there are many different ways of showing respect. It is important to use polite language, and behave with good manners. We shouldn't be rude and insult people even if we don't agree with them. Listening to others is a key part of being respectful, and just being kind to people. And remembering to say thank you is very important, in my view. It is easy to say please and thank you to people, and it makes a big difference to how they feel.

M: What are the best ways to teach children to behave with respect?

F: Well, the best way to teach children anything is to demonstrate the behaviour that you want them to copy. I strongly believe that's the best way.

M: Why?

F: It seems to me that children copy what adults do, and if you tell them to do one thing but you behave differently, they will learn from your actions, not from what you say. I think children should learn about respect in school, so teachers and other children should show respectful behaviour. They should also see this from their parents. So all adults must treat children with respect.

M: Thank you, Rosa. That's the end of the test.

Boost Your Score

Listening (pages 34–36)

 Exercise 1a

When travelling around the city of Selwyn Springs, there are a variety of transport options to consider. There is an excellent tram service which goes from the airport outside the centre to the heart of the shopping area. Other than that, there are a number of different bus routes, taxi ranks throughout the city and an excellent network of bicycle lanes, as well as a rail network with several train stations located in the city and its suburbs.

 Exercise 1b

1 If you're staying here for a week or more, there are some excellent places to visit. We would strongly recommend going along to the bike hire point and taking the brand new cycle path to the museum, where you can easily spend a day looking round. The beach is of course an essential destination for visitors, and don't forget the stunning river and waterfall, which has lovely views. You'll ideally need a car to get to the coast, while the river is accessible by rail from the central station.

2 This area is popular with young people, families and the older generation alike, as there is a lot for people of every age to do here. For those of you who have come with your children, you'll find it easy to get around the city. Our local taxi drivers are friendly and efficient, and the city buses are easy to use. Most families with little ones tend to prefer the trams to get around though, as they are spacious, clean and welcoming to all.

3 You might fancy going slightly further afield, and taking a trip out of the city. If that's the case, look out for special offers on tickets, particularly if you can be flexible about when you go. The main coach company in this area has recently started running cheap deals if you travel before ten in the morning, while many of the ferry companies offer a 'two for the price of one' deal on trips to the surrounding islands throughout this month. You'll also be able to get a discount on train tickets when you travel on Wednesdays.

 ## Exercise 2b

You will hear two students called Hannah and Tom talking about their course in sports medicine.

F: Tom, how are you finding the course so far? Are you keeping up with the workload?

M: Er, yes, I think so. I've got a few things to do before my tutorial next week, such as some reading from the list of books we were given. How about you?

F: Well, my next tutorial isn't until a few weeks' time, but I've done all the reading on the key historical turning points in sports medicine that we were told to do. I've got to go and interview a physiotherapist, and I think I've found someone who is a leading authority on sports injury, but I won't have time to do that before I see our tutor. I do need to finish writing my essay though, I'm trying to get that done in the next few days.

M: Good idea, I've just been working on that too. I'm giving a presentation tomorrow, so I also need to finish that. Did you see the other student presentation yesterday?

F: Yes, I did. I thought it was OK. The only thing I wasn't sure about was the fact that he left out one or two key points I thought, about injury prevention in top athletes, and I also thought he went on for too long overall.

M: Hmm, I didn't have a problem with the amount he said to be honest, but I agree that there were some quite significant features that weren't included and should have been. I had a problem with the diagrams he showed too, I couldn't follow a lot of them.

F: Oh, I thought they were pretty clear and helpful. Have you started thinking about your project yet? You're making a video about runners, aren't you?

M: That's right. I haven't done much yet. I'm not really sure how I'm going to organise it at the moment. I think I need to have another chat with our tutor as I have a few queries.

F: Really? Well, if you go to the course website, there's a really good discussion page there and lots of examples of similar projects that you can watch. I found that a lot more useful than talking to the others on our course, which was what I did first.

M: OK, thanks, I'll try that. I wanted to ask you, have you heard about the new funding programme in sports medicine that's being set up this year?

F: Yes, I did hear about that, it sounds like a positive move, although it seems surprising, considering the lack of investment into research these days.

M: I know! I hope future studies will benefit from this, although I suppose these things happen gradually at first.

F: Perhaps, but I'm sure it'll lead to some serious improvements in understanding how to treat sports injuries.

M: I suppose the boost in funding has come from the growing recognition that exercise is relevant to everyone. It improves the health of society in general.

F: Absolutely. Now, what did you think about that lecture about Dr Crow? She was a real pioneer of the industry and so interesting to hear more about. I hadn't realised that

she started as a receptionist and changed jobs several times before becoming a doctor.

M: Yes, she was certainly unconventional in that respect. I'd read about her before, but I didn't know about the medical centre she founded, which is still a leading institution today.

F: That was new to me too. And all the more impressive when you remember that she was not a very good student when she was younger. Actually I was surprised the lecturer didn't mention that.

M: No, you're right, he didn't.

 ## Exercises 3a and 3b

I know many of you are interested in a trip to the forest on Saturday. We'll be going on a coach and leaving at nine o'clock in the morning, so be on time, please. The weather forecast is quite promising, so no need to bring raincoats, but swimsuits would be a good idea as there's a lake you can go in if it's warm enough. For those of you with children, there should be plenty to do, including a tour by a guide, who will give a little presentation about the trees and animals in the forest. Oh, and I should mention that there'll be a picnic too, but the food is provided, so just make sure you all bring a bottle of water with you.

 ## Exercise 4

Good afternoon to all of you and welcome to Knights Language School. My name is Sarah, and I'm going to give you some information about the school and your course.

First, let me tell you about what's happening this week. The first thing on the timetable was a short exam to test your language ability, and you all should have done that this morning. On Tuesday there'll be an opportunity to find out lots of useful information as you'll be able to speak to some of our past students and ask for their advice, and the following day, we're inviting you all to an event to celebrate all the different nationalities and cultures there are among you, so put that in your diary for Wednesday afternoon.

As for the courses, they all run on slightly different dates. First of all is the reading course, which starts next week, and that goes on for twelve weeks, all the way up to the twentieth of October. Then the listening course begins in a few weeks and lasts a little longer, finishing at the beginning of next year, and for those of you taking the speaking course, always our most popular, that doesn't start until the first week of October, so you've got a while to wait.

Not all of you will choose to take exams, and that's fine, but if you want to, then you need to follow the correct procedure. All exams have a fee, and it's up to you to make sure you've paid that fee in full, otherwise you won't be able to sit the exam. There's no particular rush, but it must be paid a week before the exam dates in eight months' time. Once you've started your course, you'll need to consult your teacher and he or she will let you know which exam you can take according to your level. Then the teacher can complete an enrolment form for you and pass it on to our exams administrator.

Now we ask for a hundred per cent attendance on the courses, but we know that things can sometimes come up, and you may need to miss a class. In that case it's really important that you let us know as soon as you can. The best way to do that is by calling us and either speaking to someone or leaving a message. If you can't do that, you could tell one of the students in your class, but that's not always as reliable. Then if you've missed something really important, your teacher might want to organise a tutorial to catch up, but that depends on each case.

(Pause)

So let's talk about your first lesson. On the first day of every course, you'll need to be issued with a student card, and it will be essential to have this with you whenever you are in the school. In order to create your card, your photograph will be taken by our library staff on the first day, so be prepared for that. All our classrooms have dictionaries for you to share, but there aren't always enough for one each, so it would be a good idea to bring one along if you have your own. Oh, and please remember to submit your application form, once you have completed it, online to our office staff. You need to do that in the first week. Finally, don't forget the basics – teachers are never impressed by students who arrive in class without their pens and pencils, and you don't want to get off to a bad start!

Boost Your Score

Speaking (pages 42–43)

 Exercise 1b

Talk 1

F: I am going to talk about a present that I gave to my friend. The present was a necklace, and I chose it because I saw it and I knew she'd like it. Er… the necklace was made of silver with a flower pattern and I think it was a good choice for my friend because she wears it often. I bought the necklace from a small shop in the town centre, and I chose it because it was her birthday and she likes jewellery, and it was very pretty. She seemed very happy when I gave it to her, so I think it was a good present. Um… my friend is called Jane and I have known her for about five years. Jane and I work together, and she is one of my best friends.

Talk 2

F: I am going to talk about a present that I gave to my friend. My friend is called Jane and I have known her for about five years. Jane and I work together, and she is one of my best friends. Er, the necklace was made of silver with a flower pattern and I bought it from a small shop in the town centre, and it was very pretty. and I chose it because it was Jane's birthday and she likes jewellery. She seemed very happy when I gave it to her, so I think it was a good choice.

 Exercise 2a

The hobby I enjoy most is painting, which is something I have been doing since I was a child. I started painting at school in art lessons and I enjoyed it very much.I had a good art teacher who helped me and she made me want to be an artist, but I wasn't good enough for that! Anyway, these days I still paint as a hobby, in fact I did some painting a few days ago. I find it very relaxing so I often paint when I feel stressed, for example, when I have a lot of work to do or I am preparing for exams. As for how often I paint, well, probably about once or twice a month, because I am busy with my studies these days.

 Exercise 2d

An important moment in my life was when I got a new job last year as a shop assistant in a bookshop. I love books. Furthermore, I enjoy reading. Consequently I have always wanted to work in a bookshop. In addition, before the new job, I worked in a newsagent's. I didn't like working in the newsagent's due to the fact that it was boring.

Practice Test 2

Listening (page 44)

 Section 1

You will hear a telephone conversation between the organiser of a running club and a woman who wants to join.

First, you have some time to look at questions one to four.

(Pause)

You will see that there is an example that has been done for you. On this occasion only, the conversation relating to this will be played first.

M: Good morning, can I help you?
F: Hello, I'd like to speak to someone about joining the Rabbit Running Club, please.
M: I can help you with that. If you can give me some details I'll fill an application out for you. What's the name?
F: My name's Grace, Grace Taylor.

The woman's surname is Taylor, so Taylor has been written in the space. Now we shall begin. You should answer the questions as you listen because you will not hear the recording a second time.

Listen carefully and answer questions one to four.

M: Good morning, can I help you?
F: Hello, I'd like to speak to someone about joining the Rabbit Running Club, please.
M: I can help you with that. If you can give me some details I'll fill an application out for you. What's the name?
F: My name's Grace, Grace Taylor.
M: OK, Grace, so the next thing I need to know is when you were born, please.
F: I was born in nineteen eighty-five, on the eighteenth of September.
M: OK, I just need the year thanks. Did you say nineteen eighty-four?
F: Five, not four.
M: Right, sorry, thank you. And could you give me your address, please?
F: Well, I've just recently moved to West Horton, so I'm not far from where you meet now. I'm at number sixty-three Dittons Road, that's D-I- double T -O-N-S.
M: Got it. And that's in West Horton of course, yes, you're just round the corner from where we meet up, so that's handy. Could you give me a contact phone number then, please?
F: Sure, I'll give you my home number. It's four six eight, no wait, that's my old number, sorry, it's four seven nine, eight double six.
M: … double six. And is there an email address we can take?
F: Yes, that's gtaylor at talkmail dot com.

M: And would you mind telling me about your job? You don't have to but we like to have the information in our records so we know what kind of people join.
F: Oh that's fine, I'm a nurse.
M: I'll make a note of that then, thanks.

Before you hear the rest of the conversation, you have some time to look at questions five to ten.

(Pause)

Now listen and answer questions five to ten.

M: So have you done much running before?
F: Not a huge amount, but I started over a year ago, and I suppose I run about five times a month. I want to run more often, which is why I want to join.
M: Well, I'm just wondering which group would be best for you. We have three groups, one for beginners, one for intermediate, and an advanced.
F: Hmm, I certainly wouldn't consider myself advanced. I'll go for intermediate, unless you think I'd be better in the beginner's group…
M: Well, they're just starting out really and I think it would be too basic for you.
F: OK, fine.
M: And is running the only exercise you do?
F: No, my husband does a lot of cycling in the evenings, so I've started playing with a basketball team while he's out. Apart from that, it's mainly running that I do.
M: Great. Do you have any health or fitness issues that might affect your running?
F: I sometimes have a feeling of soreness in my knee. It's my left one, and I get pain after I've been running, but not every time, and it's nothing serious.
M: OK, well, that might be something our coach could have a look at and try to help you with.
F: That would be great.
M: Now, when you join, you'll get one of our club t-shirts – it's in red with a logo of the club on the back. I just need to know what size you think you'll need – small, medium or large?
F: Oh I think small as whenever I wear anything medium sized it tends to look too big.
M: OK, that's almost everything. I'd just like to ask where you heard about us?
F: Oh, I'm not sure if I can remember, let me think… it might have been my neighbour, he's a runner… no actually I was talking to my dentist and he mentioned you. He's one of your members, although I can't remember his name at the moment…
M: Don't worry, that'll do.
F: I did have one other question – one of my sons is interested in running and I think he might like to come. Is there a minimum age?
M: Well, most of our runners are over eighteen, but we do have a couple of younger ones – how old is he?
F: He's just had a birthday and he's thirteen now. My younger son is eleven and he's very sporty, but he's not so into running.
M: OK, I think that should be fine, but I'll make a note about it and let you know. Would you prefer me to call or email you…

Practice Test 2
Listening (page 45)

 Section 2

You will hear part of a talk by a member of staff at a country house to a group of volunteers.

First you have some time to look at questions eleven to thirteen.

(Pause)

Listen carefully, and answer questions eleven to thirteen.

Good afternoon and welcome to Pollham House. Thank you so much for coming to volunteer with us over the next few weeks. Today I'm going to give you a little more detail about exactly what kind of work you'll be doing with us and how you will be grouped for that time.

Firstly, we have group one, and you'll be meeting a lot of our guests as when they have finished looking around the house and gardens, they are encouraged to pop in to our gift shop and purchase postcards and other souvenirs, and you'll be assisting the staff there.

Moving on to group two, this team has been allocated a couple of tasks. During the first part of the morning, we'd like you to help with tours of the house, and then for the busiest hours around the middle of the day, you'll be based in our popular tearoom, providing drinks and snacks to customers. We have a small team of employed staff in there who will show you around and explain what to do.

Finally, we have group three, and in answer to feedback from some of our visitors, we've decided to increase the number of guides leading tours of the grounds. That's where you'll be helping – informing and answering questions from the public.

Before you hear the rest of the talk, you have some time to look at questions fourteen to twenty.

(Pause)

Now for the rest of you, who are not in those three groups, I'll just give you a bit more detail about some of the events that you will be helping out with.

There are several events taking place over the next few months. First of all we have our very popular history tours. Before you are expected to lead any of those you'll be given plenty of training about the history of the house and gardens, as well as some material to read to prepare yourselves. As these tours often involve a lot of questions from the guests, we've reduced the maximum number in a group from twenty to sixteen, so that should be quite manageable we hope. At first you'll be giving the tours in twos, just until you feel completely confident.

Another event you could be involved with is helping out with visits from surrounding schools. These can involve a range of age groups and number of visitors in the groups, but they are fun to do and we usually have at least one of these visits a week.

In the main hall, we are delighted to be able to put on regular musical performances. These are usually classical recitals from extremely accomplished musicians. If you are asked to work there, you'll have the opportunity to hear the music for yourself of course, and your tasks will be to check tickets of guests coming in, but also to take care of the musicians – making sure they have food and drink and anything else they need.

As well as music, we also have some wonderful art exhibits. Paintings, drawings and sculptures are on display for a week at a time in our gallery area. As the artwork is all available to buy, we'll need some volunteers in that room to meet visitors and distribute price lists as requested. You will also be expected to take orders from buyers.

A new event which we've recently started is our workshops. These are teaching events aimed at adults and have proved popular. We usually need more people to help prepare materials for these workshops, and they could be looking at all kinds of topics such as painting, for example, or another popular one recently has been sewing. They are all based on objects and history in the house.

Finally we also have the occasional special event, which are just one-off days. An example of this is our annual festival, which we have been hosting for the last three years. On that day, all of you will be required to leave your usual tasks and duties, and we'll tell you all where we need you. One of the places where we need lots of volunteers then is the car park, as we have so many extra visitors on that day, and they need to be shown where to go, and which path to follow up to the house and gardens.

Well, thank you for listening…

Practice Test 2

Listening (pages 46–47)

 Section 3

You will hear two history students discussing an assignment on medicine in the nineteenth century.

First, you have some time to look at questions twenty-one to twenty-five.

(Pause)

Listen carefully, and answer questions twenty-one to twenty-five.

M: Maggie, we really should talk about our assignment on medicine as we've still got quite a bit left to do.
F: OK, Dan, and we could share what we've found out about so far too.
M: So, the focus of the assignment is developments in medicine in Europe and America in the nineteenth century, and we started by looking at the early eighteen hundreds. It was interesting to see how many developments there had already been in the seventeen hundreds, such as vaccination and the effective use of plants to treat illnesses.
F: Yes, but from our current perspective, medical practice was still very primitive at the start of the nineteenth century and in fact some very basic techniques continued to be used. Later that century, we can see that a huge amount of change took place in a short period of time…
M: That's true. Wasn't that time period the focus of your presentation?
F: Yes, and I looked at medical science in detail. I must admit, I struggled to get a good variety of examples to illustrate the points I made. My tutor said it was fine though.

M: I thought it was really clear in the way you went from one argument to the next. It was logically planned and coherent. And I thought some of your visuals were quite unusual.
F: Thanks! Yes, the tutor commented on that and said the freshness of the imagery was a real strength.
M: Oh great, well, I can pick your brains on that topic then! Mine focused on hospitals and how they changed in the 1800s.
F: Yes, I remember. I did some reading about that too, and it was shocking to see how few beds they had in hospitals before the number was suddenly increased at the end of that century.
M: Yes, and the lack of funding was quite significant as hospitals began to take fee-paying patients who could afford to subsidise others. I was really struck by the way that specialist hospitals began to gain popularity in the medical profession, especially when the idea had previously been dismissed by many.
F: Mmm… the growth in children's hospitals and places designated to treat certain diseases was surprising after what had gone before.
M: So we've both got plenty in our notes about hospitals. Moving on to the start of the nineteen hundreds, I think it's fair to say that the profession of being a doctor had really started to be considered more respectable.
F: Well, to some extent, but that was only just beginning and still had a long way to go in my view. It's certainly true to say that there had been huge progress in surgical techniques by that time, but there can be a tendency to exaggerate improvements elsewhere – disease was still rife in many urban areas into the nineteen twenties.
M: Oh, I think you're down playing the progress a bit, but I do agree with you about methods for medical procedures.
F: Well, I've decided that for my essay on the causes of medical progress, I'm going to focus on issues such as rivalry between scientists and the motivation they had to help sick relatives and so on…
M: Ah, the social factors. That's an interesting area. I was thinking of writing about the industrial revolution, as all the inventions that were developed in that period were fundamental to medical progress, or maybe the headway made in scientific knowledge.
F: There's certainly a lot to be discussed about the importance of research into physiology and chemistry and understanding how to fight disease. If you want my advice, I think you should look more closely at that.
M: Right, I think I will, thanks.

Before you hear the rest of the conversation, you have some time to look at questions twenty-six to thirty.

(Pause)

Now listen, and answer questions twenty-six to thirty.

F: Would you mind discussing which books would be useful for our essays? I have looked at all of them, but it'd be useful to share our views and see whether we agree.
M: Fine, good idea. The one I liked the most was the book by James Pinkerton. I think that although it doesn't really contain anything new, it does give you a good general overview of the subject.
F: Yes, I thought much the same thing, but didn't you think it was perhaps a bit too general?
M: I thought there was enough evidence to support the conclusions.
F: OK. I actually thought the Maria Saville textbook was excellent. Did you read that one?

M: I did, and although it was written a long time ago, I found it useful. But I'm not sure how much bearing it has on the subjects we're researching…

F: Yes, I suppose there are other works that are more directly related to the area of our essays, like the book by Bruce Daniels, for example, which I looked forward to reading, but I must admit, I didn't read much of that one in the end.

M: Nor me, I found it lacked coherence. I just kept losing track of the point he was making.

F: I felt the same, and I thought some of the examples given were unhelpful.

M: The book by Ellen Minton was easy to read. I wonder if it had enough fresh ideas to be useful for our essays.

F: I thought there were some quite ground-breaking suggestions, but for me it really didn't go into sufficient depth in terms of reasons and causes of development. Didn't you feel that?

M: Mmm, I suppose you're right, although I liked the style of writing.

F: Then finally there was the collection of reports by Deborah Dey. I found myself disagreeing with some of her opinions, although I did think she included reference to a wide variety of subjects, which I liked.

M: Yes, although not all of it was necessarily useful for my essay. I just thought she often came to decisions and made judgements that were not backed up by the statistics. That made it difficult to accept the arguments posed.

F: Absolutely, I thought that was definitely a weakness. Anyway, that's all the books, so we need to get started soon…

Practice Test 2

Listening (page 48)

 **Section 4**

You will hear a professor in animal behaviour giving a talk about recent research on koalas

First you have some time to look at questions thirty-one to forty.

(Pause)

Now listen and answer questions thirty-one to forty.

My talk today is about the well-loved Australian marsupial, the koala, and in particular some recent research and its very interesting results. Over the last few years, fear has been growing about the reduction in the numbers of koalas in the wild, and there have been calls to protect various species of trees that koalas live in, but that issue is not what initially prompted this particular study. Instead it was part of a large research project on rising global temperatures and the consequences for animals in Australia.

Of course it has long been recognised that the diet of koalas is almost exclusively made up of leaves from eucalyptus trees, and we also know that they use these trees for shelter, in fact without eucalyptus trees koalas would soon die out. Now with this study, researchers have discovered that the acacia tree is equally important to their survival, although it performs a different function in koalas' lives. This was something we had not previously been aware of.

To begin their study, scientists attached radio collars to koalas in south eastern Australia, and tracked them at different times of year. Observations were made about their activity before climate data was measured with a portable weather station. In order to monitor differences in temperature, infrared cameras were used, and on analysing the images, the experts saw immediately that the koalas were using the cooler trunks of the acacia trees to reduce their own body temperatures. This was new information about how koalas were dealing with extreme heat – using tree trunks as a kind of natural air conditioner.

(Pause)

The team of American and Australian scientists studied about forty koalas in total and continued to make new discoveries. During the hottest periods, they saw how the animals would sit themselves around a tree's trunk, where they could be cooler, rather than on smaller branches which were warmer, so the position of their bodies in the trees determined how much relief from the heat they could obtain.

Although koalas in different regions of Australia have different thicknesses of fur, it is also known that all koalas have thicker fur on the back with less over the stomach area. For this reason it is this part of their body that they push against a tree on the hottest days, to enable them to transfer as much heat as possible from themselves to the tree.

As the koalas were tracked over time, it also became apparent that they behave differently at different times of the year, so while in the summer, they moved towards the bottom of the trees for the cooler parts of the trunk, the greater abundance of leaves near the top of the trees led the koalas to spend more time there in winter.

So why do koalas choose to cool down on acacia trees rather than eucalyptus trees? Well, the acacias are simply better adapted to stay cool. It is thought that they pull a lot more water up through their roots than the other trees, and this travels up into their trunks, branches and leaves, cooling them down.

Acacias also stay cool because they are covered in green bark and release oxygen and moisture during the process of photosynthesis. Heat from the plant's exterior causes the moisture to evaporate, and this leads to the plant cooling. This process is of course comparable to the human body and the way that sweat is used to regulate our temperature.

As referred to at the start of my talk, the future of koalas in the wild continues to look bleak. They are rapidly losing their habitat due to rampant human activity, as trees and forests are felled in aid of local agriculture and industry, and with the expansion of cities, they are also under threat from developments in housing. As their populations become isolated, the areas where they can roam for food and shelter are reduced.

As a result the usually timid animals are forced to cross into areas populated by humans to find trees, and this brings further dangers to koalas. Attacks from dogs and other pets are common, and because koalas tend to be most active at night, they run the risk of getting struck by passing vehicles as they are not easily seen in the dark. It is of course vital that the destruction of the koalas' natural habitat is tackled in future years to preserve the future of the creatures.

Practice Test 2

Speaking (page 61)

 Part 1

F: Good afternoon. Can you please tell me your name?
M: My name is Takeshi Saito.
F: And where do you come from, Takeshi?
M: I'm from Japan.
F: Thank you. Now in the first part of the test, I'd like to find out a bit about you. Let's talk about dancing. Do you like dancing?
M: Well, I am not a very good dancer! When I was a child, I learned some traditional Japanese dancing, but I haven't done that kind of dancing for a very long time. Nowadays, if I go out with my friends and we go to a club, sometimes they might dance, but I don't really join in. I usually prefer to chat with friends. I suppose I don't like people seeing me dance because I don't think I am good at it!
F: How important is dancing in your country?
M: Ah, we have a long tradition of dance in Japan, as part of our cultural history. In traditional theatre, music and dance were used to tell stories, so dancing has always been very important. However, these days, young Japanese people enjoy many different kinds of dancing, not just the traditional kind, so for example, American style hip hop dance is extremely popular in schools now, and children take part in competitions with this modern type of dancing. I think it is popular because it is good fun and kids think it is cool, you know? So dancing is definitely important in Japanese culture.
F: Do you enjoy watching dance performances?
M: Er, I don't know… well… I am not really very interested in watching people dance, and it's not something that I do very often.
F: Why not?
M: Well, it's just not something that interests me. When I was younger, my sister went to a dance class after school and sometimes her group did shows for their parents and I had to go and watch. But for me, it was a bit boring – I'd rather see a play in the theatre, or go to the cinema and watch a movie.
F: Is there any style of dancing that you would like to learn how to do?
M: Ah, that's a question I haven't really considered before. Well, as I said before, I am not a good dancer, so I suppose it would be good to have some proper lessons and learn how to dance. I would enjoy dancing if I was a really good dancer, so I think I'd like to try hip hop lessons. It would make me feel more confident when I'm out with my friends, perhaps.

Practice Test 2

Speaking (page 61)

 Part 2

F: In this part of the test, I'm going to give you a topic to talk about. You should talk about the topic for one to two minutes. You have one minute to think about what you are going to say and you can make notes if you want to. I would like you to talk about a time when you learned to do something difficult.

(pause)

F: Remember, you should talk for one to two minutes, and I'll tell you when the time is up.
M: The most difficult thing I have ever tried to learn was to play a piece of music on the piano. When I was seven years old, I started taking piano lessons, and I enjoyed it as I made progress quickly, and then by the time I was sixteen years old, I was a very good piano player. I passed all the piano exams that I took, and then my piano teacher asked me to take part in a concert. I was very excited, because she wanted me to play a beautiful piece of music, a piano concerto. However, when she gave me the music I realised it was very difficult – much more difficult than the other music I had learned to play. But I loved the piece and I wanted to play it at the concert, so I knew I had to try to learn it. Er… how I learned to do it… well… I worked very hard. I practised every day for several hours, especially the most difficult parts of the piece, which I just repeated over and over again until I could get them right. I think I spent about five weeks just focussing on that piece of music and ignoring my school work! When the day of the concert arrived, I was still very very nervous, but I managed to play the concerto quite well. I think I could have done it better, but it wasn't too bad, and I felt relieved when I had finished. Has it been useful to me…? Well, it was useful for the concert, and I suppose it was also a good process for me to learn that anything is possible if you work very hard, and that practice makes perfect.
F: Thank you. Do you enjoy learning new things?
M: Yes, I like learning, although I don't always enjoy working very hard! I like the feeling of achievement when I succeed at something.
F: Thank you.

Practice Test 2

Speaking (page 61)

 Part 3

F: Now, let's talk about learning difficult things in general. What can people do to stay motivated when trying to learn difficult things?
M: …to stay motivated… well… it is not always easy to stay motivated, especially when you have to work very hard for a long period of time. I think it is very important to set yourself a clear goal, and understand how you are working towards that goal, so maybe you give yourself some smaller targets every day or every week. Keeping your focus on the goal is important, so when I learned to drive, for example, I kept thinking about how happy I would be to get my driving licence, and that motivated me to keep learning. I also think a positive attitude is essential, so you don't feel like giving up when you are struggling.
F: Has the development of technology made learning easier?
M: Well, it depends. For some things, yes, and I suppose the internet helps us to have so much information at our fingertips all the time, which is fantastic. We can save time going to a library or looking in a book by just looking online instead. But I think that to learn something properly, it is still necessary to work hard. Learning a language for example – we still have to remember vocabulary and learn grammar and practise speaking

and so on. We can use some apps and websites for information, but we still have to work hard and study.

F: How important is it to have support from other people when trying to learn difficult things?

M: Oh, very important! When you are working hard, you need your friends and family to understand that you are busy, so you can't always be sociable. And it can be really helpful if they can be kind to you and do little things like bring you a drink or a snack, or do some other jobs, like cleaning or something, so that you don't have to do it.

F: I'd like to talk about success and failure now. What are some of the different definitions people have of success, such as money, a good job and so on…?

M: Well, I suppose the traditional concept of being successful is about being rich, living in a big house with a big car and having a good job… but these are not the only definitions of success, so for some people it might be more important to have a happy family life, to have a good circle of friends, and generally to be happy in life. In my personal opinion, these things are equally as important as a good job and money. Everyone is different, and each person's definition of success depends on their personal goals.

F: Do you think it's necessary to experience failure to become successful?

M: That's a very interesting point of view, and I think that, yes, it is true.

F: Why?

M: Well, every successful person has experienced failure at some point before they have experienced success, and they learn from the failures, what they need to change and how to improve. If you have never experienced failure, then perhaps you have never tried to do anything difficult. I think we learn from our mistakes, and failure will make us stronger and better at what we do.

F: Thank you, Takeshi. That's the end of the test.

Boost Your Score

Listening (pages 62–63)

 Exercise 1a

When you come into the offices, you will come in through the main entrance. You need to make your way to our reception, which is a large room on the right. Just before the doorway you'll see on the wall a painting of a big tree.

Then you need to speak to one of our reception staff and they will take you to meet the manager. His name's John Clarke, that's C-L-A-R-K-E, by the way. He'll be waiting for you in the meeting room.

You'll all be given an interview with a panel of three interviewers, and then we've asked all candidates to prepare a presentation, as you know. Please make sure that you stick to the guidance on timing – you need to make sure that your presentation is longer than ten minutes, but it is essential that you do not run over the maximum limit of twenty minutes, as we need to fit everyone in.

The interviewing process lasts all day, and we've got three candidates in the morning, and three in the afternoon. At lunch time we'll only have time for a short break to eat, so everyone really needs to be punctual.

After all the candidates have been interviewed, the board will get together to discuss their decision and then each candidate will be contacted individually. We hope that everyone should know the decision in two days – by Thursday, that is.

 Exercise 3b

The sight of wind turbines has become increasingly common in recent years as the demand for renewable energy grows ever greater, and we all recognise huge rotor blades across the skyline as a sign of a wind farm. However, what goes on inside the main body of the turbine, or 'nacelle' as it is called, is less well-known.

The basic procedure is that the kinetic energy of the wind is captured by the turbine and converted into an electric current, which flows through a cable that runs down the inside of the turbine tower. A transformer sits at the foot of the tower and changes the electricity into a higher voltage, ready to be transmitted to nearby buildings.

As the wind blows, it causes the rotor blades at the top of the tower to spin around, and they turn a drive shaft, which is a long cylinder. The speed of the shaft can be regulated by the gearbox, located inside the body of the turbine. A generator immediately behind the gearbox takes the kinetic energy from the spinning shaft and converts it into electric energy.

The entire top part of the turbine, that is the blades and the nacelle, can be rotated to face incoming wind in order to capture the maximum amount of energy. This rotation is controlled by a motor, mounted at the base of the nacelle, on top of the tower.

Now at certain times, it may be the case that wind speed exceeds that which can be used to capture energy, with the potential to damage the turbine. In the case of high wind speeds or turbulence, a brake can be applied to stop the rotors turning or to maintain a safe speed of rotation. This is located inside the nacelle, close to the blades.

The turbine is fitted with a device to measure wind, whose technical name is an anemometer. It collects data about wind speed as well as direction, and can be found to the rear of the nacelle, on the far side from the blades. The data is then used to inform the positioning of the nacelle and blades. The anemometer is on the outside of the nacelle.

 Exercise 4

You will hear a student called Brian and his tutor, Dr Murphy, talking about a series of lectures.

M: Dr Murphy, I wanted to ask you about the lecture series coming up next month – have you got time to talk about it now?

F: Yes, of course. Are you planning to go to many of the lectures? It would be great if you could…

M: Well, I'm quite busy, but I was hoping you could recommend which ones might be more useful as I can't attend them all.

F: Right, well, I'd definitely recommend the first speaker, Dr Sally Martin. I've known her for several years and she's an excellent speaker. She became quite famous last year when she published her book, *Examining the Sky*. It sold thousands of copies and is now regularly recommended to students.

M: Yes, I think I've read it actually, well, I've definitely heard the name before.

F: You should have read it last year because it was on the reading list! The book describes a long period of research Dr Martin did into the sun, and her findings from that.
M: But that's not what she's talking about in this lecture, is it?
F: No, the book did very well and she did a lecture tour to advertise it last year, but she's moved on to new work now. The talk she's giving as part of this series has two main topics, which are observing stars and exploring space.
M: That does sound like something I'd be interested in, as it relates to the project I'll be doing next term.
F: Perfect. I think you'll enjoy it. And I'm not the only person who values Dr Martin, other colleagues often praise her for her original work.
M: And are there any other lectures on the programme you'd particularly recommend?
F: Er… yes, there's a lecture on physics by Professor Peter Vent – do you know him?
M: I don't think so…
F: He's based in the United States and is employed as a researcher at the Space Centre in Washington.
M: Oh right. And what is he speaking about in his lecture?
F: I'm afraid I don't know exactly what it's about, you'll have to check the programme details. But whatever it is, it's bound to be popular, so you might need to book a place in advance.

Boost Your Score

Speaking (pages 70–71)

 ### Exercises 1b and 1c

1 One of the main reasons is that in western countries, a lot more women have careers. This means that they might choose to wait longer before having children because they don't want to take a lot of time off. Another reason is improved science and medical care for older mothers.

2 Well, I agree with that to some extent. I do think the government should offer financial help to retired people, especially when they have spent years working and paying taxes. However, it's also true that families should take care of their older relatives too, and the best option is for several generations to live together.

3 There are several significant differences. When my parents were children, they used to spend a lot of free time at home, whereas children today have more activities geared towards them, such as going to a soft play centre. For older children, there are other differences, the main one is technology. Young people are always on social media or their phones so they communicate in completely different ways than in the past.

4 I don't know for sure, but I think that in the future, young people might stay living at home for longer, and share houses with their parents and grandparents. If house prices continue to increase, this will be the only option for many people. I doubt that there will be any huge changes – people will probably continue to marry and have children.

5 Hmm, I think that's an interesting and complicated topic. Personally, I believe that if grandparents or even great-grandparents can live with their families, then that's the ideal situation, but this is not always possible. In my view, I suppose a home can be a good option for older people, as long as it's well run and has high standards of care.

 ### Exercise 2a

1

That's an interesting question. Well, my little brother is twelve and he watches about two hours of TV every day. I think that's too much, because when I was younger I watched a lot less than that. Nowadays I do watch quite a lot of TV though, and I don't think it's a problem for me or my nephew.

2

Hmm, well, I think there are several issues to consider, such as inappropriate programmes showing violence, which could be bad for children, and also the problem of lack of exercise when children spend too long in front of a TV. But it's also true that TV can be educational, so perhaps it depends on which programmes children watch.

3

Well, children do enjoy watching TV. I think it's an easy way to keep them entertained, and give their parents a break. I suppose there are disadvantages, like it stopping them from doing homework, but in general TV can be a relaxing hobby and sometimes children can learn from it.

Practice Test 3

Listening (page 72)

 ### Section 1

You will hear a conversation between a student and her tutor about work experience.

First, you have some time to look at questions one to five.

(Pause)

You will see that there is an example that has been done for you. On this occasion only, the conversation relating to this will be played first.

M: Hi Magda, have you come to talk about your work experience?
F: Hello Mr Clayton, yes, I wanted to ask you to go through the possible placements that are available.
M: Sure. OK, well, I've got the list here and there are four different placements you could choose from. Now, the first one is working in a shop.

The place of work is a shop, so shop has been written in the space. Now we shall begin. You should answer the questions as you listen because you will not hear the recording a second time.

Listen carefully and answer questions one to five.

M: Hi Magda, have you come to talk about your work experience?
F: Hello Mr Clayton, yes, I wanted to ask you to go through the possible placements that are available.
M: Sure. OK, well, I've got the list here and there are four different placements you could choose from. Now, the first one is working in a shop.
F: Right, and I suppose that involves dealing with customers.

M: That's right. It's a women's clothes shop, so you need to advise people sometimes on what suits them, and sell the clothes.

F: And what are the hours of work? Is it weekends?

M: Er, there may be some weekends, but in fact it just says that most of the work is mornings, and it could be any day of the week. Would that be good for you?

F: I think so.

M: There are a couple more details here – they are looking for a person who is confident, as they need someone who can be sure of themselves with their customers, and there is a start date given here too. It's quite soon actually, it's this coming Saturday.

F: Hmm, I'm not sure I'll be able to do that as I still have exams to prepare for. Can you tell me about the next placement you've got on the list, please?

M: Of course, let me see… yes, this one is based in a local restaurant.

F: Oh, what type of place is it?

M: It doesn't say which one it is, but I think it's an Italian place.

F: OK. So is that working as a waiter, managing the dining area…?

M: No, they actually want someone to help out in the kitchen, as an assistant so you wouldn't be having much to do with the public in this one. I'm not sure whether it's cooking, preparation or cleaning up.

F: Hmm. What are the work hours like?

M: Well, they want someone there from eleven in the morning until three o'clock in the afternoon, and that's Mondays, Tuesdays and Wednesdays, so the hours are quite short actually.

F: And whereabouts is it?

M: It's on the other side of the city from college – the address is Brook Street, and apparently that's not far from the station, so you should be able to get there quite easily. They also say that you don't need to have any particular experience as the work is fairly basic and they can teach you what you need to do.

F: That's good, but I think the hours are a bit too short.

Before you hear the rest of the conversation, you have some time to look at questions six to ten.

(Pause)

Now listen and answer questions six to ten.

M: How about working in a hotel? That's the next place on the list.

F: Perhaps, it depends on the type of work. Is it dealing with guests in reception?

M: Actually the main responsibility is to assist the manager. That could involve a range of duties, couldn't it?

F: Yes, I like the sound of that. What are the hours like for that one?

M: Well, when I phoned the hotel to arrange this, the woman I spoke to said it would be six evenings every week, but she contacted me again later to say that it would actually be five.

F: Right, that would be fine.

M: She did make a point of saying that they consider punctuality to be extremely important, and that the person working with them would have to make sure they were always on time for work. She was very strict about that!

F: I could do that. Is that the last one then?

M: No, there's one final opportunity, and it's a placement for work experience in the large new garage on the High Street. Do you know the place I mean?

F: I think so. I remember when it opened a few weeks ago. The trouble is I don't know anything about that field of work.

M: Well, don't worry, perhaps you don't need to – they are looking for a person who is prepared to take on duties in the office.

F: Oh, well, I should be able to do that. What are the hours like for that one?

M: It's afternoons, so they want someone from twelve o'clock until five pm, and that's from Monday to Friday. You might like that as it's a good amount of work each week…

F: Yes, it sounds good. Are there any particular requirements for the position?

M: Just one thing – they are keen to stress that they want a person who is always smart, as the job involves meeting people from other companies. Being knowledgeable about the work is not necessary, though, as they are willing to provide training.

F: Great, thank you.

M: So what do you think…

Practice Test 3

Listening (page 73)

 Section 2

You will hear part of a radio programme about a family festival that will take place soon.

First you have some time to look at questions eleven to thirteen.

(Pause)

Listen carefully, and answer questions eleven to thirteen.

M: Good morning everyone, and welcome to the show. Later we'll be talking to some school children about a project they've been doing, but first we've got Jane Piper – one of the organisers of the Dalbree family festival to tell us all about what's happening there this weekend. Thanks for coming in Jane.

F: Hi! I'm going to tell you about some of the fantastic things to do at the festival, and where to find everything you need. The festival goes on all weekend, but first, I'd like to tell you about what we've got happening on Saturday. We'll have several activities going on for families. Last year we had a very popular cookery workshop organised by a group of school teachers, and children made pizzas and salads. The same group of teachers is coming back to the festival this year, but this time they've decided to focus on handicraft classes, including painting, sewing and pottery. At ten o'clock there's a great opportunity for kids who are interested in sport. We'll have a football trainer from the Dalbree sports academy who can help budding young strikers with their goal-scoring. If you want to sign them up for that, go to the field next to the tennis courts. At the same time, we'll be running our usual dance session for adults – an hour of practice followed by a short performance. That's really designed for the parents, so please come along! During the afternoon, there'll be some great taster sessions in various adventure sports. We've got a climbing wall, which is always good fun, and that's completely free for anyone over the age of sixteen to have a go at. Alongside that, we'll have our archery site for those of you who want to practise using a bow and arrow. There's plenty of equipment provided for all sizes, strengths and abilities so the whole family can have a try.

Before you hear the rest of the programme, you have some time to look at questions fourteen to twenty.

(Pause)

Now I'm going to talk about some of the events taking place on Sunday.

In the corner of the park, you can find our mini arena, where we'll have a quiet, relaxing atmosphere for our poetry reading. Authors with a range of styles will be talking and reading from their work throughout the morning. Get there before midday if you want to catch that, as the arena will be closed after that.

We've got a big café tent full of food stalls to cater for all kinds of tastes and requirements, but if you prefer to bring your own lunch, there will be a designated area for picnics, so do come along, especially if the weather is poor. You'll be able to find food from a huge range of countries and types of cuisine, but particularly good value are the sandwiches and rolls, and the ice cream vendors tend to reduce their prices too, especially later in the day.

I know a lot of people are looking forward to seeing some wonderful theatre performances on the central stage, and so am I! This always attracts large crowds, so make sure you check the sign located near the entrance to the stage to find out about the show you most want to see, and get there ten minutes before it is due to start if you can.

The Music Zone will be located on the east side of the park this year, not far from the lake. As always, we've got a fantastic line up of bands and singers performing music from jazz and country to rock and pop. There will be a stall in the Music Zone selling bottles of water, but we'd ask people in the audience not to have food inside this section, as it can get very crowded. Again, this is an attraction that is equally popular with all ages, so make sure your children come along.

In the long field, there will be a wide range of sporting competitions taking place throughout the day. Along with the chance to try a long jump contest, we'll also have several races such as a sprint, a long-distance run and an obstacle course.

Finally, don't miss our gallery. In this area, you'll have the chance to see some truly wonderful pieces of art, all produced by local painters and sculptors. If you see something you like, of course most of the work will be available to buy, so remember to bring your wallet!

Practice Test 3

Listening (page 74)

 Section 3

You will hear two students called Rob and Emma discussing their project on young people and technology.

First, you have some time to look at questions twenty-one to twenty-four.

(Pause)

Listen carefully, and answer questions twenty-one to twenty-four.

M: So Emma, we need to finish our project about young people and technology…

F: Yes, OK. Let's look at the results of our research. Now we were planning to only look at young people in work originally, weren't we?

M: Mmm, but then we changed it to concentrate on students, and I think that was the right choice.

F: I agree. So we just need to make that focus clear in the title of the project. Now, have we got enough information about everything? I wondered if we needed more facts and figures on computer gaming…

M: Mmm, no I think we've got more than enough on that actually. But there's definitely a gap in our research on the use of social media, don't you think?

F: Oh yes, you're right. OK, I agree, we need to get more data on how people use social media then.

M: Great. So how shall we go about getting that information? We could conduct a survey – that worked well before.

F: But that's rather time-consuming and we're in more of a hurry now.

M: Or how about we do it by email? That's quicker.

F: I think we should try telephone interviews – that'll take much less time.

M: Great idea! So is there anything else we need to do more work on? We should decide exactly what to work on next so we can get started soon. After we've finished today, maybe we should look at our presentation – that still needs organising?

F: Yes, I think the written report can wait until we've collected all the research. So I agree with you.

Before you hear the rest of the conversation, you have some time to look at questions twenty-five to thirty.

(Pause)

Now listen, and answer questions twenty-five to thirty.

M: Let's look at some of the detail in our notes about mobile phone use and check we've got all our facts and figures straight.

F: OK. I thought it was really interesting when we asked people how they'd feel if they lost their mobile phone – of course the vast majority said they'd panic that they might not keep up to date with things they needed to know…

M: Yes, but a few – about 6% I think – actually said it would give them a sense of freedom and take some pressure off! Quite a surprising result. Personally I don't think it would bother me too much…

F: Really? I think you'd struggle without it! And what did you have listed as the reasons people gave for having a mobile phone?

M: Well, almost everyone mentioned staying in touch with friends and of course being able to go online and use the net at any time, but apparently the key for most of us is being able to contact people if you're running late or if you have an emergency, that sort of thing.

F: Right. And because most young people have their phones with them all the time, they can use them to help with all sorts of tasks, like homework.

M: Yes, and it's great that instead of having to make a trip to the library, we can check things so much more quickly and easily on our phones without even having to leave the room!

F: But when we compared the data, I noticed that in fact it takes young people even longer nowadays than it did their parents to get their work done. I suppose that's because they aren't always concentrating on the task.

M: Well, you know what the studies say about getting things done – all that focus on your phone means there's not enough space left in your brain for problem-solving.

F: Yes, and we've got that example to include in our report about how you can spend all evening stuck on a problem, then the next morning in the shower, a great idea pops into your head.

M: Mmm, and while it may feel as though the water wakes you up and gets your brain going again, the point is that you're not influenced by technology and your imagination can just run free, allowing room for new thoughts to occur.

F: Right.

M: It's not surprising really, but there were a few things that did surprise me, like the amount of times young people check their phones – about 150 times a day according to our research!

F: Yes, but I was aware of that already just from myself and my friends. It's clear that young people spend many hours each day in front of a screen too, but I hadn't realised that the average teenager sends over 3000 texts a month.

M: Mmm, that was unexpectedly high. How about you? Do you think you rely on your phone too much yourself?

F: I must admit, I do get excited whenever my phone beeps to let me know there's a new message, and that's the trouble – it's hard to ignore so it can stop you getting on with other things.

M: Yes, and it's always a sign that you've got plenty of mates, isn't it?

F: It's not that so much, but rather the expectation of something new and fun – before you actually read a message, there is so much potential for what it could be!

M: I suppose so…

Practice Test 3

Listening (page 75)

 Section 4

You will hear a lecturer in travel and tourism giving a talk about airline compensation.

First you have some time to look at questions thirty-one to forty.

(Pause)

Now listen and answer questions thirty-one to forty.

Good morning everyone. This morning I want to talk to you about a controversial issue in the travel industry, which is compensation. Specifically, compensation for flight tickets when planes are delayed or cancelled.

A case has recently been brought to my attention of a flight by the budget company, Bolt Airlines. There is a lot of data available about this particular case, particularly because while the scenario was playing out, comments were being made about what was happening on social media, by both passengers and airline staff alike.

This case was of particular interest as there were a variety of problems that occurred. The initial problem was on the ground in the airport itself, as a technical issue made it impossible for customers to check in. This caused a delay to the flight that lasted five hours.

That flight then took off for its destination and landed safely, but then there were problems for the return flight of the same plane. After passengers had boarded the plane, a fault was discovered with the lighting, which required an engineer to be called out. The engineer failed to resolve the issue, and after more waiting, the chances of the plane departing were ended as the airport was closed until the following morning.

Although the passengers may have been ready to fly, there are of course strict regulations about the amount of rest the crew need to have before flying, and this prevented the flight from being rescheduled early in the day. There were no staff free to replace the crew, because the whole incident took place during a public holiday, and all staff were already deployed.

There was one further problem still to come – as the flight crew were being driven from their hotel to the airport, their vehicle became caught up in a road accident, which left two crew members in hospital. Eventually the company chartered another plane to come and pick up the passengers, but by this time, their departure was thirty hours late.

(Pause)

So let's look at the rules of compensation in the travel industry. What inconvenienced passengers are entitled to is dependent on the length of the delay up to a point, but the rules also take into account the flight distance. Generally speaking, however, the airline should at least provide food for passengers who have been waiting for over three hours.

If flights are cancelled, passengers can be entitled to a good sum of money, but not if the circumstances are considered to be extraordinary, or outside of the airline's control. A common example of this would be bad weather, for instance. Additionally, compensation is unlikely if enough notice is given for a cancellation.

Although there are some sound regulations in place to protect passengers, my own research and that of others has found that people often start a claim for compensation but find the online system for doing so extremely complicated. This complexity leads many to give up, which is a real problem for travellers who are entitled to a fairer system.

Now, how should these issues be addressed? Well…

Practice Test 3

Speaking (page 88)

 Part 1

M: Good afternoon. Can you please tell me your name?

F: My name is Maria Silva.

M: And where do you come from, Maria?

F: I come from a small town in Brazil.

M: Thank you. Now in the first part of the test, I'd like to find out a bit about you. Let's talk about drawing and painting. How often do you draw or paint a picture?

F: Hmm… well… I'm not very good at either drawing or painting, and in fact I don't think I am very talented at any kind of art in general, so I hardly ever draw or paint properly. I suppose the only time I draw pictures is when I am doodling for no reason, so hardly ever.

M: Do you enjoy looking at art in galleries or museums?

F: Oh yes, I do. Even though I am not an artist myself, I really enjoy looking at art by talented people, and I appreciate good painting. In the city where I live now there is a great gallery of art and I love going there and looking at the paintings, the sculptures, photographs, everything…

M: Why?

F: I suppose it makes me feel relaxed, and looking at beautiful things makes me feel happy too.

M: Do you think children should learn to draw and paint at school?

F: That's a difficult question, because I'm not sure whether being artistic is something that can be taught. As someone who doesn't have much artistic talent, I didn't really like art lessons at school, because I found it very difficult, and I always compared what I did with other pupils. However, I think it is important for children to learn about art, and to get an appreciation of the arts in general, so I suppose it depends on the content of the lessons.

M: Would you ever buy a drawing or painting by someone else?

F: Absolutely, yes. In fact at the moment I have got a painting in my house hanging on the wall that a friend of mine did, although I didn't pay for it! She gave it to me as a present, and she is a gifted painter and I love the painting. Generally speaking, art can be quite expensive, so I have never bought anything by a professional artist, but I hope that I will in the future. I think it is important to have beautiful things in your home which suit your personal taste.

Practice Test 3

Speaking (page 88)

 Part 2

M: In this part of the test, I'm going to give you a topic to talk about. You should talk about the topic for one to two minutes. You have one minute to think about what you are going to say and you can make notes if you want to. I would like you to talk about a news story you read or heard about that made you happy.

(pause)

M: Remember, you should talk for one to two minutes, and I'll tell you when the time is up.

F: OK. My topic is about a positive news story, and it took me a while to think of one, but then I remembered something that I heard on the radio a few weeks ago. It was a report about a region in India where hundreds of thousands of people participated in an amazing project where they planted trees. Apparently the country made a pledge to improve the size of forests and the amount of trees in India at a meeting on climate change, and as part of this, officials gave out millions of baby trees to be planted in one particular state.

Most of the people who helped were volunteers, and I think it was a world record for the most number of trees planted in twenty-four hours, although I can't remember how many trees it was altogether. On the news report, they said that this will help to improve the air quality in India, which causes big health problems, and hopefully it also helped to raise awareness about environmental issues.

I heard this news when I was just listening to the radio and I wasn't really concentrating, but as the reporter described the story, it caught my attention, and I thought it was really interesting.

As for when the story happened, well, I'm not entirely sure, but I think it wasn't long ago, as it was on the radio quite recently.

And, um,… the reason why it made me happy was that I am very concerned about the environment and the many problems facing our world. Usually when there is a story in the news about the environment, it is a negative one, about an accident or a study of pollution or climate change. So it was really inspiring to hear a positive story about a group of people working together to do something good, to help the whole planet… um…

M: Thank you, Maria. And do you usually pay attention to what is happening in the news?

F: Yes, I do. Knowing what's going on in the world is very important to me, so I tend to look at news online several times a day, and I also listen to the radio when I am cooking at home. I usually listen to news programmes instead of music so that I can stay informed.

M: Thank you.

Practice Test 3

Speaking (page 88)

 Part 3

M: Now, let's talk about news around the world. How important is it for individuals to know about what is happening in the world?

F: I think everyone should be aware of events in countries all around the world. As I mentioned, personally I try to keep up with the news, and I really believe that as individuals, we all need to know what is happening. In this way, we can understand the world better, and if there are things happening that we want to change, we need to know about them in detail. Of course events around the world can affect us personally, so it is important to be up to date with them, if there are changes to laws for example, that's something everyone needs to know about because it can impact every individual's life.

M: Is local news more important for individuals than global news?

F: Hmm, that's hard to say. Perhaps it is in some ways because it's about where you live, and obviously that might affect you more directly. For instance if a new shop is opening, or even closing down, that can be important to know. But on the other hand, local news stories can be less significant, and things happening on the other side of the world might have more of an effect on us, such as climate change. So I think both can be important.

M: What is the best way to find out about local news?

F: That's more difficult, isn't it, because international news is more available online and on TV. I guess the best way is to watch local news programmes on TV, although that's not always easy to find. Another idea would be to buy a local newspaper, yes, that's probably best because there are local papers in every town, and they usually have a lot of detail about the area and local events.

M: Let's talk about media controls now. To what extent should we believe the news stories that are on the internet?

F: Well, it really depends which website you are looking at. Um, there are some news websites that I definitely trust more than others, and they are the ones that are linked to TV channels or newspapers. Of course we have to be careful because there are fewer controls on the internet, but to be honest, a lot of stories in some newspapers turn out not to be true anyway. So it isn't very different. We all know that anyone can make something up and put it in a blog, so those kind of stories should not be trusted but it just depends on the website in my view.

M: Whose responsibility is it to ensure that we can trust news on TV and in newspapers?

F: Well, I suppose some people think that it is the responsibility of the government, but I don't agree with that.

M: Why not?

F: Because I don't think the government should be involved with the media at all. If they have any control of the media, then the news becomes biased. Er, so I think it is down to the individual responsibility of the owners of TV channels and newspapers. If they check that the stories they publish are true, then the public can trust them, and that will make them more popular. If they can't be trusted, then people will stop buying those papers or watching those channels. That should be enough to guarantee self-control.

Practice Test 4

Listening (page 89)

 **Section 1**

You will hear a conversation between a woman who wants to buy some office furniture, and a man who works for a furniture company.

First, you have some time to look at questions one to five.

(Pause)

You will see that there is an example that has been done for you. On this occasion only, the conversation relating to this will be played first.

M: This is Quest Office Supplies, how can I help you?

F: Oh, hello. I'd like to order a couple of things for delivery, please.

M: Of course, I can help you with that. My name is David and I'm a sales assistant. I'll take you through your order today.

The man's job is sales assistant, so sales assistant has been written in the space. Now we shall begin. You should answer the questions as you listen because you will not hear the recording a second time.

Listen carefully and answer questions one to five.

M: This is Quest Office Supplies, how can I help you?

F: Oh, hello. I'd like to order a couple of things for delivery please.

M: Of course, I can help you with that. My name is David and I'm a sales assistant. I'll take you through your order today.

F: That's great, thank you. So the first thing I'd like to order is a new office desk. I've seen one in your catalogue that I like. It's on the cover in fact.

M: Ah, yes, I know the one you mean. It's called the Solar desk, S-O-L-A-R, is that the one?

F: Solar… sorry… is that E-R or A-R?

M: A-R.

F: Lovely, thank you. And can you tell me what that's made of? Are the legs made of metal?

M: Let me just check. Ah, we do have some made with metal legs, but this one is entirely built from wood and plastic. They are the only materials in the desk.

F: OK, well, that's fine. I need it to go in my home office actually, and the room is quite small so I suppose I ought to check the measurements with you before I place the order.

M: Of course. So looking at the details here, I can tell you that the width is fairly short, just one point two-five metres, and the depth of the desk is fifty-three centimetres, so it should fit in most work spaces.

F: Yes, that's going to be perfect for me. And what's the height of the desk?

M: The standard is usually around seventy centimetres, but this one is just a little higher at seventy-four, so I hope that will be suitable.

F: That sounds fine. And I was wondering whether there is anything else in a similar style to go with the desk? I need a new chair if there is one that matches?

M: Er, no we don't have that, but there is a lamp in the same style if you're interested in that?

F: No, I don't think so, thank you.

Before you hear the rest of the conversation, you have some time to look at questions six to ten.

(Pause)

Now listen and answer questions six to ten.

F: The other thing I wanted to order was a new printer. I saw one in your catalogue too – it's the white one on page thirty-eight.

M: Ah yes. I'll give you the model number so you can make a note of it, it's M-3-5-5-X.

F: OK, got it. Yes, that's the one I wanted.

M: That's from a new range and is very good value. All our printers come with guarantes, and these new ones have a twelve month guarantee, so if you have any problems during that period, you can bring it straight back and get a replacement.

F: Oh good. So I'd like both items delivered to my home, please.

M: Yes, they can both be delivered together. The soonest date we have available is 2nd August – is that OK for you?

F: Oh, I'll be on holiday then, in fact I'm coming back that day. How about the third?

M: Yes, that would be fine. 3rd August then.

F: Can you tell me what time they'll arrive?

M: Well, we don't usually give a specific time at this stage. But you can find out on the day if you check the website. It'll show you where our drivers are and see when they are due to get to you.

F: Great. And how much will that all cost, in total?

M: Well, delivery is free, the desk is eighty-five pounds and the printer is thirty-two pounds, so that's a hundred and seventeen pounds altogether.

F: Fine.

M: Now, I'll just need your address and credit card details…

Practice Test 4

Listening (page 90)

 Section 2

You will hear part of a radio programme about classes taking place in a community.

First you have some time to look at questions eleven to fifteen.

(Pause)

Listen carefully, and answer questions eleven to fifteen.

M: This morning I'm delighted to welcome Judy Clark from the Hamilton Learning Programme. That's an organisation that arranges classes and workshops in a huge range of subjects for adults in the local area. Welcome to the show, Judy.

F: Thank you.

M: I understand you have some information for us about the timetable of classes organised for the next three months.

F: That's right, I just want to tell your listeners about some changes to the programme for this term, and give them information about how to apply. Let's start with the Drama club on Mondays. That's been running for about five years now and it has become by far our most popular class. For this reason, we're adding an extra evening, so from next term, there will be two groups, on Mondays and Wednesdays.

Moving on to our next change, last term we started running language lessons on Tuesdays, and they've proved to be a great success. If you have an advanced level in a language though, this group isn't for you, the lessons are aimed at beginners only for the time being. As I mentioned, we have already had a couple of successful courses, and they were lessons in French and Spanish, so we're branching further out this month with the brand new addition of Chinese lessons. We're very excited about these because we haven't been able to run them until now.

Another of our recently added courses continues on Thursdays, and that is a course of singing lessons with local performer and teacher Danielle Bedham. She welcomes anyone from the age of sixteen upwards to come along, and a lovely aspect of that class is that there are regular opportunities to take part in concerts so you can invite your friends and family to come to those.

Finally, another new course is starting on Saturday mornings. That's a group where you can learn baking, including how to make decorated cakes. Those sessions are going to be aimed at families, so all ages can attend, and parents are encouraged to bring their children along. As the course is new to our timetable, the first session is going to be completely free, so why not try and see if you like it? You'll still need to sign up beforehand though, and places will be limited to twenty at first.

Before you hear the rest of the programme, you have some time to look at questions sixteen to twenty.

(Pause)

Now, if you like the sound of any of the classes I've mentioned, or if you fancy finding out more, please do go to our website to find out more. You'll find the full timetable there, and you can have a good look and decide which class to do and which day to attend.

The classes can fill up quickly, so it's a good idea to get in touch as soon as possible to check availability of the class you want to do. Just email our administrator, whose address is on the website, to find out if there are places left.

At the same time, you ought to check the details of the course you're interested in. Some of the courses are just for fun and to help you achieve new skills, but others are associated with exams that you can take if you want to, so you should know about that before you sign up.

You will receive a reply to your email, and be asked to pay a deposit for the course fees at this stage. The prices of each course can vary from around seventy to about a hundred and thirty dollars, depending on the length and type of course, but whatever course you choose, you will be expected to pay ten per cent as a deposit.

As soon as you have done that, you will be sent a letter in the post. This will contain details of your course booking, and as well as that you'll get a handbook telling you all about our organisation, with details of where to go on the first day and information about our staff and so on.

Finally, the one thing left to do will be to pay the full amount of the course fees. If you prefer, you can pay them as soon as you book, which could be anything up to eight weeks before the start date, but it is essential that the full balance is paid one week before your first lesson.

Then you'll be ready to come along and enjoy your course.

M: Well, thank you very much, Judy….

Practice Test 4

Listening (page 91)

 Section 3

You will hear a conversation between a student and his tutor about a presentation on coastal erosion

First, you have some time to look at questions twenty-one to twenty-six.

(Pause)

Listen carefully, and answer questions twenty-one to twenty-six.

M: Hello Doctor Matheson. Thanks for making time to see me. I wanted to check a few things with regards to my presentation.

F: That's fine. So I've asked your particular group to give presentations on the topic of coastal geography, but you should all target different areas within that topic. Which sub-topic have you chosen?

M: Well, my first thought was to look at erosion, and now I've spoken to the others in my group I've decided to stick with that. From the planning I've done so far I think it'll be long enough, but I've just rearranged some of the content to make it clearer and I'm happier with that now.

F: Good.

M: I wanted to check with you exactly what is essential to include. Do you think it would be helpful to present a case study of a particular local area to give a clear example of how the coast is affected?

F: That could be an idea, but what I really think you need to think about is a way of exemplifying the effects of the sea and demonstrating just how 'constructive' and 'destructive' waves influence the coastline. You could also mention the power of wind, but I would keep that brief, you don't need to show it visually.

M: Right, I'll make a note of that, thanks. I've done quite a lot of reading and research already, but are there any particular books you would recommend?

F: Hmm, there's nothing in particular that springs to mind, but I think you should consider whether there are any gaps in your knowledge that you need to address.

M: Well, I've got some texts on the differences between chalk and clay that I haven't read in detail, so I could look at that…

F: But do you need to discuss that in your presentation? You don't need to go into much detail on types of rock so it may not be worth your time. Perhaps you could read up on seawater and how the acids it carries can dissolve rock.

M: Yes, I agree that's important, but actually I've already spent a lot of time on that topic.

F: OK, well, another thing to focus on is cliffs and how cracks appear in them – have you prepared much on that?

M: Maybe not enough, so yes, I think I need to read up more on that.

F: Good idea. Have you been sharing your ideas with the classmates in your group as you go?

M: We talked a lot when we were first planning, but not so much recently. I think I need to chat to one of my group about how to best integrate imagery and diagrams because I could do with some advice about that.

F: Fine, but I would also recommend that you communicate with each other about what you're actually going to include because you all have a wide topic area to discuss and it's vital that you avoid any overlap of content.

M: Yes, of course. I'll make sure we do that.

F: Have you given many class presentations before?

M: No, just one really. I gave a presentation to the class last term. It went quite well, but the tutor on that course had a few areas for me to improve. I had to learn a lot of jargon related to the topic, and perhaps because of that, I felt nervous. I tried to have confident body language but I got the feedback that I rushed my speech, which made it hard to understand.

F: I see. So that's obviously something you'll need to work on this time – make sure you address that in your preparation.

M: I will. Thank you for all your advice.

F: You're welcome. By the way, how did you find the seminar given by the geologist from the museum? I hope it was useful for everyone.

M: Oh yes, it was very good. Some of my classmates weren't too sure about having to work in groups for some of the tasks, but I thought that although he occasionally veered off in different directions, the delivery of the material was engagingly done and we were all rather gripped by that.

F: That's good to know, I'll pass that on.

Before you hear the rest of the conversation, you have some time to look at questions twenty-seven to thirty.

(Pause)

Now listen, and answer questions twenty-seven to thirty.

F: Before you go, I should give you the details of the field trip next week. You are going aren't you?

M: Oh yes. I'm looking forward to doing some practical work based on the theory we've discussed in class. A minibus has been organised hasn't it?

F: Yes, we're hoping to leave at half past nine so make sure you are at the library in good time as it will depart from just in front of there, and we'll go straight to the beach.

M: That's fine. Do we need to bring anything in particular? I suppose I should bring something for lunch…

F: Actually, we'll probably stop in a café so there's no need to carry food or drink. One thing that would be useful to have is a torch if you've got one – it can be hard to make things out without one. Of course you should all bring a pencil and notebook for sketches and notes.

M: Right, I'll pass that on to the others. I'm hoping to get a chance to have a really close look at the top and the bottom of the cliffs and to find specific evidence of the features we've looked at on the course.

F: Yes, and not only will you be able to do that, but there will also be time to explore the beach to collect samples, and you can investigate the local caves too. That should be particularly interesting.

M: Great. And then I think we're going to meet someone who does volunteer work at the coast?

F: That's right, a coastal warden. He's going to be available to talk about coastal activity in general and the work he does to help protect the area. You can also find out more about what they're doing to control the damage done by the sea and a wall which is currently being built along the seafront.

M: Well, thank you very much again…

Practice Test 4

Listening (page 92)

 Section 4

You will hear a student presentation about an artist called Jasper Johns.

First you have some time to look at questions thirty-one to forty.

(Pause)

Now listen and answer questions thirty-one to forty.

For my presentation, I have chosen to focus on the work of the artist Jasper Johns.

Jasper Johns was born in the state of Georgia. After his parents separated, the young Johns went to live with his grandfather in South Carolina. His first access to art was noticing pictures of animals in countryside scenes, which he believed had been painted by his grandmother, and which were displayed in the homes of several relatives.

At the age of six, Johns remembers a visit to his town from a travelling artist, and this was clearly an experience that encouraged the beginnings of his interest in art. The visiting artist stayed at his house, and spent his days painting decorations on the mirrored walls of the town's Greek café. According to Johns, the artist had a very large collection of brushes and paint, some of which Johns then took to experiment with. The artist discovered the theft and demanded their return!

In the early nineteen fifties, Jasper Johns moved to New York City, where he fell in with a group of other artists and creatives, some of whom were questioning the place and purpose of art at that time. They believed that art should be abstract, and a pure expression of emotions, while Johns disagreed, and was of the opinion that art must represent what is real, and reflect familiarity in the world.

However, despite his clear views, Johns struggled to find his personal artistic voice. He became tired of waiting to become an artist and decided he needed to do something drastic in order to become one. To this end, he took the unusual decision to destroy all the works of art he had created up to that point and to start again, setting out to develop his own style.

One night in 1954, it is said that Johns dreamed of painting the American flag, and on waking, he felt inspired to do so. He recreated the symbol in one of his most famous works, called *Flag*. Instead of a conventional canvas, the artist chose to paint on a surface of newspaper, which allowed print and stories to show through, connecting the image of the flag with a particular time and place.

For this work and many others of his, Johns used a type of paint known as encaustic, which is a mixture of paint and wax. This enables the artist to use sculpting techniques as well as painting, and gives the picture a raised texture.

Another well-known piece by Johns is *Target*, painted in nineteen fifty-five. As with *Flag*, he painted several different versions of the same symbol, changing them slightly each time. The image of concentric circles is intended to represent the human eye, so the painting simultaneously draws the viewers' attention while seeming to look back at them.

(Pause)

Johns prefers to leave brushstrokes and drips of paint visible on his works' surface, as a reminder that although his pieces can look manufactured, they are in fact handcrafted. By leaving evidence of his technique, Johns draws attention to his presence as the artist in each work. As well as flags and targets, over 180 of Johns' works, in mediums ranging from painting and collage to prints and sculpture, depict numbers as the subject.

But why might an artist choose to represent something so commonplace? Well, this again allows Johns to shift the focus away from the image to the technique used to create it. Unlike many artists, Johns does not depict people in his work, as such a portrait will inevitably provoke an emotional response to its subject.

Johns' work from the nineteen fifties remains his most popular, and in the nineteen eighties, two of his works from the fifties were sold for record-breaking sums. Since the eighties, he has typically produced only four to five paintings a year, some years producing none at all. The large-scale paintings he has created are much favoured by collectors and due to the fact that they are quite rare, they are difficult to acquire. In twenty thirteen, one report named Johns as the thirtieth most valuable artist in the world.

Practice Test 4

Speaking (page 104)

 Part 1

F: Good afternoon. Can you please tell me your name?
M: My name is Stefan.
F: And where do you come from, Stefan?
M: I come from Poland.

F: Thank you. Now in the first part of the test, I'd like to find out a bit about you. Let's talk about weather. What's your favourite type of weather?
M: I really like warm weather, and for me, warm weather is around twenty-five degrees or more. Anything below that is too cool, and when the temperature is above thirty, it can be too hot. I don't mind rain but I am really not keen on strong wind – that is the kind of weather I do not like. I like to feel comfortable, and for me, the most comfortable weather is warm and calm.
F: What is the weather usually like in your country?
M: The weather in Poland is quite warm at the moment. During the summer, it usually reaches around twenty-five degrees Celsius – that's probably the maximum temperature – but in winter it can be very cold and we get a lot of snow. In the summer, there can be a lot of rain too, especially in July. I don't mind the rain, but I'm not keen on snow. I prefer warmer weather to the cold winter days.
F: What kind of activities do you enjoy doing in good weather?
M: When it is not too rainy, I really like walking around the city. Sometimes I meet my friends, and we go out together – we wander around and visit cafés and shops. That's a relaxing way to spend my time I think. I also have a bike, and I like cycling. It's good exercise and it makes me feel as though I have a lot of energy.
F: Does the weather affect the way that you feel?
M: Hmm, I've never really thought about that before. I don't think it does, no.
F: Why not?
M: It's just not something that bothers me. If I am in a good mood, it has nothing to do with the weather, and even when the weather is bad, it doesn't really change my mood. I know some people say they feel less happy when the weather is very bad, but it's not the case with me.

Practice Test 4

Speaking (page 104)

 Part 2

F: In this part of the test, I'm going to give you a topic to talk about. You should talk about the topic for one to two minutes. You have one minute to think about what you are going to say and you can make notes if you want to. I would like you to talk about a possession – something that you own – that is important to you.

(pause)

F: Remember, you should talk for one to two minutes, and I'll tell you when the time is up.
M: The possession that I own that is most important to me is definitely my bike. It's not the most expensive or best quality bike, but I use it almost every day, and life would be difficult without it.

I got the bike about two years ago, and in fact it was second-hand. The bike that I had before was really old and I decided to replace it, and I found this one for sale on a website. The man who was selling it hadn't used it very much, and I think it was a bargain. Er… as I mentioned, I've had it for about two years I think, and I hope I will have it for a long time in the future, because it's still in really good condition.

The reason that it is important to me, the main reason is that I usually cycle to my work. It takes about thirty minutes, and that's much quicker than taking a bus or train, and in addition to that, it is free! I haven't got a car, so cycling is perfect for me. It also means that I can get some exercise without going to the gym, and I like being outside. The only problem is when the weather is bad. I don't mind cycling in the rain, but if it's heavy rain, I get very wet, and that's a pain because I need to change my clothes.

Apart from work, I also cycle in my free time in the summer, so my bike is my hobby as well, and I just use it all the time to get around the city quickly. If I didn't have my bike, I'd have to walk everywhere, so I'm very attached to it!

F: Thank you, Stefan. Are your possessions important to you in general?

M: Er, yes, I suppose they are. Although I'd like to think that I could live without a lot of my things, I'd prefer to have them to make life easier and more fun. Of course my friends and family are far more important though.

Practice Test 4

Speaking (page 104)

 Part 3

F: Now, I'd like to talk about having a lot of possessions. Does owning a lot of possessions make people happy?

M: Hmm. Well, I think it can help. It depends on what those possessions are – so having things like photos or anything that has been given to you by your family or loved ones – those things are really important. Life would be very tough without phones, computers, televisions, music and so on, so yes, I think there are a lot of possessions that can make people happy.

F: Is owning a lot of possessions more important to people nowadays than it was in the past?

M: Perhaps, yes…

F: Why?

M: I think that we are probably more materialistic than we used to be, and there are more possessions available to have, so in the past, most people would have owned a lot less than people do now. These days everyone has a mobile phone, most people have a TV and a computer in their house, all my friends have lots of technology for listening to music, and in general I think in our culture, young people expect to own a lot of things. So young people want to have a phone when they are ten or eleven years old, and they want to own all the same things as their friends, like trainers, new clothes and so on. I think it is part of our culture to want more things, and people enjoy acquiring more and more…

F: Let's move on to shopping and consumerism. What influences people to buy certain products? Think of advertising, celebrities and so on…

M: Oh, a lot of things. Advertising is definitely a strong influence on people, and companies spend a lot of money developing commercials for TV and posters because they know how important it is to convince people to buy their products. But obviously some people are influenced by famous stars, especially celebrities that they are fans of. I suppose that if you admire a celebrity, and you want to be like them, you might think that buying the same products

that they use can make you feel closer to them. Apart from those things, I think most people are very influenced by their friends – especially children, but adults too. If a lot of my friends have the same phone, or are wearing a brand of clothing, then I want to fit in too, and it makes me want to buy those products.

F: What are the advantages and disadvantages of a consumer culture for society?

M: I think there are a few disadvantages, such as the gap between people with money, and people without. Consumer culture can make people feel more divided. In my view, the disadvantages outweigh the advantages, as it creates a society of people who always want more and are never satisfied. I suppose an advantage could be that it increases people's motivation to work hard and make money.

F: Should the government be responsible for regulating competition among companies in a consumer culture?

M: That's an important question. Yes, I think that the government has a part to play in ensuring fairness in big companies. We have seen that these companies cannot always regulate themselves, so the government needs to step in and make sure that one company does not dominate one particular market. It is a complicated area…

F: Thank you, Stefan, that's the end of the test.

Answers

Boost Your Score

Listening (pages 6–7)

1a **a)** In order to apply for the job all candidates <u>are required</u> to have an art degree.
b) Initially, everyone believed it <u>unlikely</u> that the artist would achieve her ambitions.
c) Participation in the school trip is <u>not permitted for</u> pupils who do not have a sunhat.
d) People weren't convinced by what the professor said as <u>there simply wasn't enough</u> evidence.
e) Bus travel is available at a <u>greatly reduced price</u> for those who study full time.
f) It is planned that speaking practice will make up <u>a significant proportion</u> of every lesson.

1b Students' own answers

2a The cue is *the start date (for the language course)*.

2b **a)** historian **b)** river **c)** glass **d)** time **e)** journal **f)** proposal

2c **a)** *first published work was written in collaboration*
b) *location ... not far from*
c) *but one that particularly stands out is entirely assembled from*
d) *one of its chief benefits has been to increase the amount*
e) *many of you were unable to get hold of*
f) *before you embark on your essay, we strongly advise you to hand in*

3a **1** size **2** India **3** reflective **4** trumpet **5** plastic **6** engineer **7** moved **8** interaction

3b **1** and are <u>particularly striking</u> due to their <u>size</u>.
2 Kapoor <u>was actually</u> born in <u>India</u>,
3 The <u>surface of the sculpture</u> is <u>reflective</u>
4 <u>could be said to resemble</u> a giant <u>trumpet</u>.
5 using <u>a combination of materials</u>, chiefly a special type of flexible <u>plastic</u>
6 <u>Working in collaboration with</u> Cecil Balmond, an innovative and contemporary <u>engineer</u>,
7 <u>uniquely</u>, the deflated venue can be <u>moved</u> to a new location after each performance.
8 <u>one of the main characteristics of Kapoor's art is</u> the principle that the viewer's <u>interaction</u> with his art

Boost Your Score

Reading (pages 8–10)

1–3a Students' own answers.

3b The language is dense / complex. A summary condenses information from a text and so a lot of information is expressed concisely.
The summary makes use of paraphrases and synonyms. A summary rephrases information from the text in different ways.

4 **a)** Ragweed thrives in the increased temperatures <u>caused by global climate change</u>. (participle clause)
b) Scientists predict that the weed, <u>which is now present in Central Europe</u>, could soon reach the UK <u>where the milder climate</u> as well as the rapid reproduction <u>for which the plant is notorious</u> could mean it spreads swiftly. (relative clauses)
c) The <u>potential impact on hay fever sufferers</u> is concerning scientists. (complex noun phrase)

5 **a)** Ragweed is an invasive plant capable of producing a huge quantity of pollen <u>grains</u> in a single year.
b) Scientists are concerned at the issues raised by the <u>rapidity</u> at which the plant is spreading on certain types of land.
c) Sneezing and irritated eyes are symptoms caused by ragweed in common with other <u>types</u> of allergenic plants.
d) Ragweed pollen ... is produced late in the year, prolonging the hay fever <u>season</u>.
e) Researchers at the University of East Anglia are developing <u>strategies</u> to reduce the health risks of pollen sensitivity.

6 **a)** irritated **b)** produce **c)** invasive plant **d)** rapidity **e)** prolong **f)** hay fever sufferers **g)** allergenic **h)** the hay fever season **i)** spread **j)** affect **k)** a single

7 & 8 Students' own answers.

9 **1** affecting **2** immune system **3** sleep (patterns) **4** urban **5** lengthen

Boost Your Score

Writing (pages 11–13)

1 **a)** True **b)** False – 25% of households, not people
c) False – 4%, not 4 million **d)** False – we don't know
whether it rose steadily or sharply **e)** True
f) False – this is speculation, the reasons for the data
are not given. **g)** True **h)** False – the data given
goes up to 2011, not now.

2 **a)** increase / rise / climb / grow **b)** fall / decrease /
drop / decline **c)** remain stable / remain steady /
plateau **d)** fluctuate / waver

3 **1** b and c **2** a and c **3** a and b **4** b and c **5** a and b

4a
Sample answer

The table presents data about the popularity of five sports
in England in two different time periods, namely 2005 –
2006 and 2015 – 2016. Swimming was the most popular
sport overall, while golf was the least popular from this list.

Although swimming remained the most popular sport, the
total number of adults who swam once a week dropped
significantly, from 3.2 million in 2006 to 2.5 million in 2016.
However, athletics was only half as popular as swimming
in the first year, with 1.4 million participants, but rose
to 2.4 million in 2015 – 2016, only marginally less than
swimming. From 2005 to 2006, cycling was the second
most common sport, and although the participants
increased from 1.7 million to 2 million, it was only the third
most popular in 2016. 2 million people played football
regularly in 2006, and this fell slightly to 1.9 million after
ten years. Golf was played with much less frequency
than the other sports, and the number of participants
decreased from 0.9 to 0.7 million over the ten-year period.

4b Students' own answers.

Boost Your Score

Speaking (pages 14–15)

1 The answers are all too short.

2a **Suggested ideas**
a) which rooms I like / who I live with / the area I live
in / facilities nearby
b) supermarket shopping, why, who with / clothes
shopping, why, who with / whether I like shopping
or not
c) type of books I like / how often I read / why I like
(don't like) reading

2b & 2c Students' own answers.

2d This is not a good answer. Although the candidate
uses a good range of vocabulary and expressions,
the content is on the topic of TV, not books. The
candidate does not answer the question he was
asked.

4b **a)** Health and fitness; working together, help with
concentration. **b)** She's not sure – For: competitive
sport prepares children for the real world and
teaches them to do their best. Against: children
should enjoy sports without pressure.

Practice Test 1

Listening (pages 16–20)

Section 1 (page 16)

1 September **2** Tuesday **3** Reade **4** photo / photograph
5 573992 **6** party **7** £40 / forty pounds **8** museum
9 library **10** café

Section 2 (page 17)

11 F **12** A **13** E **14** G **15** B **16** bus **17** mountain(s)
18 (afternoon) tea **19** 31 / thirty-one **20** hike

Section 3 (pages 18–19)

21 C **22** B **23** A **24** A **25** B **26** G **27** B **28** D
29 F **30** E

Section 4 (page 20)

31 hurricane **32** metal **33** electrical **34** walls **35** cheap
36 expand **37** connected **38** scientist **39** trip / holiday
40 trees

Reading (pages 21–31)

Reading Passage 1 (pages 21–24)
Questions 1–14

1 T **2** F **3** NG **4** F **5** NG **6** T **7** T **8** breeze **9** features
10 Searchlights **11** batteries **12** (a) wire **13** clockwork
mechanism **14** dish

Reading passage 2 (pages 25–28)
Questions 15–27

15 B **16** D **17** E **18** A **19** F **20** C **21** B / E **22** B / E
23 tools **24** distances **25** fire **26** diet **27** gorillas

Reading passage 3 (pages 29–31)
Questions 28–40

28 B **29** D **30** A **31** B **32** Y **33** Y **34** N
35 NG **36** N **37** Y (The words in bold paraphrase 'famous
brand logos'.) **38** D **39** E **40** C

Writing (page 32)

Task 1

Sample answer

The two graphs present data about money spent making purchases online. The first shows a steady growth in online spending in the USA from 2010 to 2015. In the second graph, we see data for one American company between 2007 and 2013, showing the proportion of total products that were bought online. In both cases, an overall increase in online purchasing is shown.

The first graph shows that in 2010 approximately $170 billion was spent online in the USA. ~~This amount rose slightly by 2011~~ then continued to rise more sharply for the following years. Online spending increased steadily to reach just under $350 billion in 2015.

In the second graph, 29% of all purchases were made online in 2007. Online purchases increased significantly to just over 40% in 2009, but growth slowed down between 2009 and 2011. There was a ~~slight fall~~ in online sales from 2011 to 2012, but the amount of products bought online climbed again to peak at 46% in 2013.

Task 2

Sample answer

The protection of the environment is an issue that is always in the news. Air pollution is one of the key factors which contributes to global warming and endangers people's health, and one of the major causes of air pollution is the popularity of cars. I firmly believe that banning cars from city centres would be an effective measure in reducing air pollution.

Some cities have already taken the step of making their centres into pedestrian zones, and introducing fees for drivers who come into the centre. These actions have been successful in reducing pollution and I believe they should be carried out in many more cities.

Furthermore, all large cities have efficient public transport systems, which means it is very easy to travel without a car. Cities such as Tokyo, London, Paris and others have underground train systems which are fast, inexpensive and easy to use, while smaller cities are equipped with buses or trams. These would also be quicker and easier to use if cars were banned.

There are many additional advantages to banning cars, such as preventing road accidents, avoiding the problems of parked cars in the street, and increasing fitness as people have to walk more. It would also improve conditions for cyclists.

Some people claim that banning cars would restrict personal freedom, but in my view, polluting the atmosphere is a bar to everyone's freedom to breathe clean air.

To conclude, the reasons for banning cars from city centres are extremely convincing, and outweigh the arguments against.

Boost Your Score

Listening (pages 34–36)

1a tram, bus, taxi, bicycle, train

1b **1** A **2** C **3** A

1d

2

This area is popular with young people, families and the older generation alike, as there is a lot for people of every age to do here. For those of you who have come with your children, you'll find it easy to get around the city. Our local taxi drivers are friendly and efficient, and the city buses are easy to use. Most families with little ones tend to prefer the trams to get around though, as they are spacious, clean and welcoming to all.

3

You might fancy going slightly further afield, and taking a trip out of the city. If that's the case, look out for special offers on tickets, particularly if you can be flexible about when you go. The main coach company in this area has recently started running cheap deals if you travel before ten in the morning, while many of the ferry companies offer a 'two for the price of one' deal on trips to the surrounding islands throughout this month. You'll also be able to get a discount on train tickets when you travel on Wednesdays.

2a **2** What criticism do Hannah and Tom both make about a classmate's presentation?

3 If Tom has any questions about a video project, Hannah recommends

4 What does Tom think about current funding into research?

5 What surprised Hannah and Tom about the life and work of Dr Crow?

2b **1** A **2** B **3** C **4** A **5** C

3a B and D

3b

I know many of you are interested in a trip to the forest on Saturday. We'll be going on a coach and leaving at nine o'clock in the morning, so be on time please. The weather forecast is quite promising, so no need to bring raincoats, but swimsuits would be a good idea as there's a lake you can go in if it's warm enough. For those of you with children, there should be plenty to do, including a tour by a guide, who will give a little presentation about the trees and animals in the forest. There should be plenty of time for the kids to play around in the woods after that too. Oh, and I should mention that there'll be a picnic for lunch, but the food is provided, so just make sure you all bring a bottle of water with you.

4   **1** B   **2** A   **3** A   **4** B   **5** C or D   **6** D or C

5   Transcript with answers and distractors underlined

Good afternoon to all of you and welcome to Knights Language School. My name is Sarah, and I'm going to give you some information about the school and your course.

First, let me tell you about what's happening this week. The first thing on the timetable was <u>a short exam to test your language ability, and you all should have done that this morning.</u> On <u>Tuesday there'll be an opportunity to find out lots of useful information as you'll be able to speak to some of our past students</u> and ask for their advice, and <u>the following day, we're inviting you all to an event to celebrate all the different nationalities and cultures</u> there are among you, so put that in your diary for Wednesday afternoon.

As for the courses, they all run on slightly different dates. First of all is the <u>reading</u> course, which starts next week, and that goes on for twelve weeks, <u>all the way up to the twentieth of October.</u> Then the <u>listening course</u> begins in a few weeks and lasts a little longer, <u>finishing at the beginning of next year,</u> and for those of you taking the <u>speaking course,</u> always our most popular, that <u>doesn't start until the first week of October,</u> so you've got a while to wait.

Not all of you will choose to take exams, and that's fine, but if you want to, then you need to follow the correct procedure. All exams have a fee, and it's up to you to make sure you've paid that fee in full, otherwise you won't be able to sit the exam. There's no particular rush, but <u>it must be paid a week before the exam dates in eight months' time.</u> Once you've started your course, <u>you'll need to consult your teacher and he or she will let you know which exam you can take according to your level.</u> Then <u>the teacher can complete an enrolment form</u> for you and pass it on to our exams administrator.

Now we ask for a hundred per cent attendance on the courses, but we know that things can sometimes come up, and you may need to miss a class. In that case it's really important that you let us know as soon as you can. The best way to do that is <u>by calling us</u> and either speaking to someone or leaving a message. If you can't do that, you could <u>tell one of the students in your class, but that's not always as reliable.</u> Then if you've missed something really important, your teacher <u>might want to organise a tutorial to catch up, but that depends on each case.</u>

So let's talk about your first lesson. On the first day of every course, <u>you'll need to be issued with a student card,</u> and it will be essential to have this with you whenever you're in the school. In order to create your card, <u>your photograph will be taken by our library staff on the first day,</u> so be prepared for that. All our classrooms have dictionaries for you to share, but there aren't always enough for one each, so <u>it would be a good idea to bring one along</u> if you have your own. Oh and please remember to <u>submit your application form, once you have completed it, online</u> to our office staff. You need to do that in the first week. Finally, <u>don't forget the basics – teachers are never impressed by students who arrive in class without their pens and pencils,</u> and you don't want to get off to a bad start!

Boost Your Score

Reading (pages 37–39)

1   The five-storey façade of the Hawa Mahal at Jaipur

2a   **a)** Each one offers a fascinating insight into India's immense historical and cultural diversity …
b) These buildings served not just as royal residences but also as areas for public meetings called *durbars* and garrisons for troops.
c) many owners have opened their properties to paying guests
d) (giving) visitors the chance to observe at first-hand the luxurious lifestyle once enjoyed by the ruling elite
e) Jaipur was founded in 1727 by Maharaja Sawai Jai Singh …
f) It was built in the late 18th century by Maharaja Pratap Singh to provide the ladies of his court with somewhere to watch the activity on the bustling streets below without being seen.
g) The stone façade was richly decorated by stonemasons of the Rajput ruler Rawal Jaisal in the 12th century and is deemed one of the best examples of its kind in India.
h) It is now one of India's most stunning heritage hotels.

2b   **a)** The pronoun (*one*) has been replaced with a noun (*palace*). The verb *provide* is a synonym for *offer*; *interesting* is used instead of *fascinating*. Word forms have been changed: *diversity* (n) to *diverse* (adj); *historical and cultural* (adj) to *history and culture* (n); *immense* (adj) to *hugely* (adv).
b) The sentence has been reversed by using a different linking structure: (*served*) *not just* (*as*) … *but also* (*as*) has been changed to (*were for*) … *as well as* … . Specific uses (*public meetings called durbars and garrisons for troops*) have been generalised (*for public and military use*).
c) The clause has been changed from an active one (*many owners have opened*) to a passive one (*Many properties have been opened*).
d) This paraphrase makes extensive use of synonyms: *guests* (n) is a synonym for *visitors* (n); the phrase *see for themselves* acts as a synonym for the phrase *observe at first-hand* and *wealthy way of life* replaces *luxurious lifestyle*.

e) In this context, *establish* (v) is a synonym for *found* (v). The sentence has been changed from passive (*was founded*) to active (*established*).

f) *Ladies of his court* has been changed to *women from his court*; *busy* (adj) is a synonym for *bustling* (adj); *seen* has been changed with the prefix *un-*, so *without being seen* becomes *remain unseen*.

g) Some of the detail has been left out of this paraphrase, making a more concise sentence without the use of 'and'. There has been a change of word form: the past participle form of the verb (*decorated*) has been used as an adjective; the prepositional phrase *in the 12th century* has also been used as an adjective (*twelfth-century*).

h) The comparative structure of this sentence has been changed from *now one of the most* to *not many … as*; *awe-inspiring* (adj) is a synonym for *stunning* (adj).

3   **a)** Specific: fort, palace; General: building, dwelling, landmark, monument, property, residence, structure

b) crown   **c)** intricately decorated, ornate

d) celebrated = famous; 'crumbling' means that parts of the stone are breaking off; fascinating = very interesting; gargantuan = huge (the adjective 'colossal' is also used in the text); 'grand' describes a building that is large but also important and/or impressive ('imposing' and 'splendid' are used to express a similar concept) 'instantly recognisable' means that the building is very well-known; 'modest' is used as the opposite to 'gargantuan'; 'opulent' means beautiful with a lot of decoration and using expensive or luxurious materials; 'stunning' has a similar meaning to 'breathtaking' and 'awe-inspiring'; 'unique' is used to describe the façade in the Hawa Mahal because it is the only one of its kind

5   **1** E   **2** B   **3** A   **4** F   **5** C (sandstone)   **6** H

6   **7** D   **8** C   **9** A   **10** B   **11** C   **12** A   **13** B

7   Students' own answers

Boost Your Score

Writing (pages 40–41)

1a   Essay B

1b   conjunction (while); referencing (that); discourse markers (In my own view, one of the main reasons, furthermore, in addition); relative pronoun (which); conditional (if someone has committed a crime, they deserve to be punished)

2a   **a)** who – doctors (with many years of experience)
b) which – immunisation   **c)** who – photographers and journalists   **d)** where – several large parks
e) whose – politicians'   **f)** which – the claim that improving air pollution is the duty of government

2b   **1** d   **2** a   **3** b   **4** f   **5** e   **6** c

3

Suggested ideas:

I disagree that increasing taxes is the best way to reduce pollution for a number of reasons.

Big companies produce a lot of pollution from their factories, which is one of the main causes of pollution.

Because big companies produce the majority of pollution, it is unfair to punish individuals.

If petrol taxes were increased, driving and travelling by plane would be more expensive, affecting individuals but not companies.

4

Sample answer

It is a fact that nowadays the vast majority of people all over the world have access to the internet, and this development has an impact on the use of traditional books. If people can find information online, will public libraries be needed in the future?

On the one hand, libraries are already becoming less important. My local library has recently cut its opening hours and reduced the number of staff, which is because of the lack of visitors. Many people read e-readers these days, which are smaller and more convenient to use than books. In addition, students who could visit a library to research information are more likely to go online, and they can do this in their own home, or on their phone in any location.

On the other hand, there are some advantages to public libraries. Not all families have access to computers at home, and although most people have a smartphone, they are not always easy to use for finding information online. Furthermore, many people prefer traditional books to e-readers, and borrowing from the library is a good way to get books for free. Another advantage of libraries is that they can hold events for people in the community, for example story readings for children or school events.

In my opinion, public libraries are in danger, but if they were to close, it would be a very sad thing. Libraries are an important part of any community, so I hope they will continue to exist for many years.

5   Students' own answers.

Boost Your Score

Speaking (pages 42–43)

1c Talk 1 is poorly organised as the speaker moves from one point to another and then goes back again. Talk 2 is logically organised as the speaker talks about each point in turn.

2a & 2b The underlined words are linking devices, which show what sort of information is coming next and help the listener to follow the talk.

Additional information	and, for example, in fact
Cause and result	because
Contrasting information	but
Relative pronouns	which, who
Changing topic	anyway, as for...

2c **Suggested ideas:**
a) *My favourite day of the week is Saturday. I like it because on Saturday I don't work and I usually go to the park. When I am there, I enjoy walking and taking photos of the beautiful landscape. Another thing I do there is visit the café, where I often buy a drink. Sometimes I meet my friends in the café and I chat with them. In the evenings I often go out, and I go to the cinema or to a restaurant, for example.*
b) *An important moment in my life was when I got a new job, which happened last year when I got a job as a shop assistant in a bookshop. I have always wanted to do this kind of work because I love books and reading. Before the new job, I worked in a newsagent's but I didn't like working there as it was boring.*

2d Although there are some effective techniques, such as putting the first sentences together and avoiding repetition, the linking words used are too formal. *Furthermore, consequently, in addition* and *due to the fact that* are appropriate for writing, but can sound too formal for speaking.

Practice Test 2

Listening (pages 44–48)

Section 1 (page 44)

1 1985 **2** Dittons **3** 479866 **4** nurse **5** intermediate
6 basketball **7** knee **8** small **9** dentist **10** 13 / thirteen

Section 2 (page 45)

11 C **12** A **13** D **14** 16 / sixteen **15** school **16** musicians
17 price lists **18** sewing **19** (annual) festival **20** car park

Section 3 (pages 46–47)

21 B **22** A **23** C **24** B **25** B **26** G **27** A **28** C **29** E **30** F

Section 4 (page 48)

31 A **32** B **33** A **34** position **35** stomach **36** winter
37 water **38** sweat **39** housing **40** vehicles

Reading (pages 49–59)

Reading Passage 1 (pages 49–51) Questions 1–13

1 T **2** NG **3** T **4** NG **5** F **6** F **7** (rock) shelter
8 (eastern) Africa **9** 70 000 / seventy thousand
10 Nile Valley **11** (on / by) foot **12** wildlife **13** Asia

Reading Passage 2 (pages 52–55) Questions 14–27

14 viii **15** iii **16** v **17** iv **18** i **19** vi **20** B **21** D **22** B
23 C **24** acute **25** perfume **26** proteins **27** gene

Reading passage 3 (pages 56–59) Questions 28–40

28 C **29** F **30** A **31** G **32** D **33** C/E **34** C/E The references to items C, D and E are all found in the third paragraph of the passage. This paragraph mentions that O'Keeffe 'still attracts a pilgrimage of worshipping tourists, both female and male' (C & D) and that her 'best-known subject matter is the large and eye-catching flowers' (E).
35 B/D **36** B/D **37** dramatic **38** summer **39** 1940
40 symbols

Writing (page 60)

Task 1

Sample answer

The pie charts present opinions of café customers. They show satisfaction with cleanliness, staff service and choice and quality of food in January and August of one year. The greatest changes were in the choice and quality of food, which showed an increase in satisfaction levels, while the other areas showed little change.

In terms of cleanliness, most customers were happy in January and August, with over half very satisfied in both months. There was a rise in the percentage who were just satisfied, from 21% to 31%, and dissatisfied customers fell from 26% to 15%.

The number of customers who were very satisfied with staff service showed little change, but the percentage who had complaints dropped from 11% to 6%.

In January, almost half of customers were not happy with the food. However, this dropped significantly to under a fifth in August (17%), and the amount of very satisfied customers grew from 23% to 36%. The proportion of customers who were just satisfied also increased from less than a third to just under half.

Task 2

Sample answer

When I was a child, my parents both worked, and they went to their offices every day. These days however, my mother only works from home, and my father works three days at his office and two days at home. This is part of a growing trend of people working from home, and it has advantages and disadvantages.

There are several reasons for this change in work habits. The most significant reason is the development of technology, which has made working from home possible. With a computer, employees can answer emails and work online at any location. Secondly, most parents need flexible working hours, and as more women are working after having children, working from home allows both mothers and fathers to adapt their work to fit with school times.

Flexible hours is one advantage for people working from home, but there are others, such as no commuting time, convenience, saving money on food and drink as well as travel costs, and no distractions from colleagues. The benefits for employers include reduced costs on office supplies and maintenance, higher productivity and happier staff.

Nevertheless, there are drawbacks. Working at home may be lonely, and there are other distractions such as housework and TV. For employers, it may be difficult to monitor staff and to communicate effectively.

To sum up, the pros and cons of working from home depend on the job. Personally, I think it is a positive development overall, as it means more choice and flexibility, but it may not be the best choice for all jobs and all workers.

Boost Your Score

Listening (pages 62–63)

1a **a)** tree **b)** Clarke **c)** 20 / twenty minutes **d)** break **e)** 2 / two days

1b **a)** Two words instead of one **b)** Wrong spelling **c)** Not read the question / listened carefully **d)** Wrong word which sounds the same (homophone) **e)** Not read the question carefully to match the answer with the preposition

1c **a)** Check the number of words you can write in each gap and stick to it. **b)** Listen carefully to the correct spelling and write the exact letters that you hear. **c)** Read the question carefully so you know exactly what information you need. **d)** Check your spelling and use the correct word, especially if it can be spelled in different ways according to the meaning. **e)** If there is a preposition before the gap, think about what type of word(s) can follow it.

2 **Suggested answers:**
B in the north; alongside / next to a river **C** in the middle / centre of the island **D** in the north east; near a church **E** on the south east coast; on the right-hand side of the map **F** at the bottom of the island; alongside the coast

3b **1** E **2** B **3** D **4** A **5** C

4 **1** Examining the sky **2** the sun **3** observing stars **4** original **5** Space Centre **6** popular

5 Students' own answers.

Boost Your Score

Reading (pages 64–66)

1 Students' own answers.

2 All of these points are discussed in the passage, except for c and f.

3a **a)** Philippa O'Brien is quoted in the final paragraph, so the answer to this question must be there. **b)** This question tests a general understanding of the final paragraph. **c) & d)** The correct answer is **B**. Philippa O'Brien mentions a number of different issues that a new beekeeper needs to be aware of. In the final sentence she mentions the importance of people going into beekeeping 'with (their) eyes open' (= be aware of the issues of a situation) **A** is not correct: Philippa O'Brien doesn't mention numbers of beekeepers.

C is not correct: Philippa O'Brien mentions winter conditions but does not state that these are the biggest problem.
D is not correct: Philippa O'Brien mentions the exaggeration of one risk, but this does not apply to all risks.

3b **a)** This question doesn't tell you where in the article the information is. The key words in the question are eating habits, British people and granulated sugar. The information is in the fourth paragraph, where there is a sentence mentioning how much refined sugar British people eat. *(Reports indicate that the British eat a mere half-jar per year compared with a gruesome 53 kilos of refined sugar.)*
b) This question tests detailed understanding of one point / sentence.
c) & d) The correct answer is **D**. This is a paraphrase of the sentence in the text which states that in general British people eat more refined sugar than honey.
A is not correct: the expectations of the reports are not discussed
B is not correct: the effectiveness of the two sweeteners is not discussed.
C is not correct: the effect of processing on taste is only mentioned with regard to honey (not refined sugar).

4 **3** The correct answer is **B**. The writer gives statistics which show that bee numbers are down overall.
A is not correct: the writer doesn't give an opinion on whether to take up beekeeping
C is not correct: the writer mentions famous people who kept bees but not their influence on others.
D is not correct: the writer doesn't give an opinion on how long the trend will last.
4 The correct answer is **A**.
B is not correct: the writer says the opposite, ie 'it rarely occurs to us'
C is not correct: the number of blooms required is mentioned, but not that they are in short supply.
D is not correct: the taste of honey is mentioned but not compared with table sugar.
5 The correct answer is **C**. (The writer compares ways of pacifying bees.)
A, B and **D** are not mentioned in the passage.
6 The correct answer is **C**. Bee Wilson mentions that Langstroth's invention meant that the original man-made hives 'no longer had to be destroyed in order to get the honey'.
A is not correct: Bee Wilson does not specify an increase in popularity of beekeeping. She mentions the beehive led to 'a small resurgence' in our consumption of honey but that it 'did not restore the mass appeal of honey'.

B is not correct: honeycomb is mentioned but not in relation to the design of the hive.
D is not correct: the destruction of old-fashioned hives in order to get to the honeycomb is mentioned, but not as a result of the arrival of new hives.
7 The correct answer is **D**. (This paraphrases 'One of the pleasures' at the start of paragraph 6.)
A is not correct: this is not mentioned in the passage.
B is not correct: expensive honeys are mentioned but no opinion is given on their taste.
C is not correct: the writer mentions a number of different variations in taste.
8 The correct answer is **C**. Philippa O'Brien says there are no more wild honey bees, so the remaining honey-producing bees must be farmed.
A is not correct: Philippa O'Brien says a beekeeper needs to know how to 'control the diseases and pests that have recently come from the Far East' but does not mention bees from the Far East.
B is not correct. Philippa O'Brien mentions that there are no more wild bees, but not that entire species have been wiped out.
D is not correct: Philippa O'Brien only mentions that bees have no resistance to new pests and diseases from the Far East, not to pests and diseases in general.

Boost Your Score

Writing (pages 67–69)

1b

ESSAY A
Paragraph 1 – introduction
Paragraph 2 – reasons for people living alone
Paragraph 3 – advantages & disadvantages
Paragraph 4 – conclusion

ESSAY B
Paragraph 1 – introduction
Paragraph 2 – advantages to living alone
Paragraph 3 – disadvantages to living alone
Paragraph 4 – reasons
Paragraph 5 – conclusion

1c This is personal preference; both styles of organisation are appropriate.

3a **1** Personally **2** To begin with **3** In addition **4** In contrast **5** Nevertheless **6** for example **7** To sum up **8** whereas

3b **1** e **2** d **3** g **4** h **5** c **6** b **7** a **8** f

4

Sample answer

In the past, most people used to take holidays in their own countries, but nowadays an increasing number of people travel abroad. There are many reasons for this development, as well as several advantages and disadvantages.

First, a significant reason for increased international tourism is a rise in individual wealth. More people can afford to travel abroad than in the past. Moreover, we are now more aware of other countries and places in the world, due to media and the internet. Another reason is improvements in transport, which have made it quicker and easier to travel long distances.

There are some clear advantages for individuals. For instance, it is well known that travelling can be educational, and people's lives can be enriched by experiencing life in foreign countries. In addition, there is a positive result for those countries, as visitors bring money into the economy and help to create jobs.

However, there are drawbacks, particularly for the environment. As flying becomes more popular, it causes significant pollution. Furthermore, some remote places and buildings may be damaged by huge numbers of visitors coming from abroad, and tourists can even behave irresponsibly, leaving litter behind or using up resources.

To conclude, it seems that the popularity of international tourism is set to continue in the future, as it becomes easier and more affordable. In my opinion this is a positive development for individuals overall, as we can experience new places and cultures, but it is essential that tourists travel responsibly and respect the places they visit.

Boost Your Score

Speaking (pages 70–71)

1a   **a** v **b** iii **c** ii **d** iv **e** i

1b   **1** d **2** e **3** b **4** c **5** a

1c

1 One of the main reasons is that in western countries, a lot more women have careers. This means that they might choose to wait longer before having children because they don't want to take a lot of time off. Another reason is improved science and medical care for older mothers.

2 Well, I agree with that to some extent. I do think the government should offer financial help to retired people, especially when they have spent years working and paying taxes. However, it's also true that families should take care of their older relatives too, and the best option is for several generations to live together.

3 There are several significant differences. When my parents were children, they used to spend a lot of free time at home, whereas children today have more activities geared towards them, such as going to a soft play centre. For older children, there are other differences, and the main one is technology. Young people are always on social media or their phones so they communicate in completely different ways than in the past.

4 I don't know for sure, but I think that in the future, young people might stay living at home for longer, and share houses with their parents and grandparents. If house prices continue to increase, this will be the only option for many people. I doubt that there will be any huge changes – people will probably continue to marry and have children.

5 Hmm, I think that's an interesting and complicated topic. Personally, I believe that if grandparents or even great-grandparents can live with their families, then that's the ideal situation, but this is not always possible. In my view, I suppose a home can be a good option for older people, as long as it's well run and has high standards of care.

1d

Agree	I agree with that to some extent
	(Other ideas: I completely agree / I totally agree with it)
Speculate	I don't know for sure, but I think that
	If ..., this will ...
	will probably
	I doubt that ...
	(It's possible that... / ... might happen / It's difficult to say but perhaps...)
Make comparisons	There are several significant differences
	whereas
	there are other differences, the main one is
	(On the other hand... / there are many similarities / in contrast)

2a

Answer 2 is the best because it addresses the question in detail. Answer 1 is too personal, discussing the candidate's own experience rather than the issue. Answer 3 does not go into enough depth, and discusses the issue in a trivial way.

2b   Suggested ideas

a) Tax on unhealthy food / education / advertising campaigns / cheaper fruit and vegetables

b) Important: essential skill / important for health
Not important: should learn from parents / academic subjects more important

c) Yes – most people cook / ready meals are not popular / traditional food is salads and fish No – fast food is popular with young people

d) Delicious food / no cooking or washing up / relaxing. However – some people like cooking / restaurants are expensive

e) Fewer people cooking / more ready meals / less healthy / families eating around the TV / more international recipes and restaurants

Practice Test 3

Listening (pages 72–75)

Section 1 (page 72)

1 mornings **2** Saturday **3** restaurant **4** kitchen **5** station
6 manager **7** five evenings / 5 evenings **8** garage **9** office
10 smart

Section 2 (page 73)

11–13 A / C / E **14** midday **15** picnics
16 sandwiches **17** sign **18** food **19** races **20** local

Section 3 (page 74)

21 students / studying **22** computer gaming
23 telephone interviews **24** presentation **25** B **26** A
27 A **28** C **29** B **30** C

Section 4 (page 75)

31 social media **32** check in **33** lighting **34** closed
35 public holiday **36** road accident
37 (the) flight distance **38** over three hours / over 3 hours
39 bad weather **40** give up

Reading (pages 76–86)

Reading passage 1 (pages 76–79)
Questions 1–13

1 F **2** NG **3** NG **4** T **5** T **6** F **7** NG **8** face **9** breathing
10 dogs **11** genetically **12** generations **13** vaccine

Reading passage 2 (pages 80–83)
Questions 14–27

14 icons **15** BASIC / basic **16** program / programme
17 graphic **18** gaming **19** C **20** D **21** A **22** D **23** B
24 D **25** F **26** B **27** E

Boost your score! (page 83)

1b   **a)** B and F
   b) & c) Many of the paragraphs describe how
   difficult the Commodore 64 was to use but
   paragraph B describes modern computers '…*today
   as we point, click, swipe and pinch our way through
   rich graphical user interfaces…*'
   The topic is referred to in F '…*in an age where our
   computers require no understanding of underlying
   architecture or components*' but this is not a description,
   so B is a better answer.

Reading passage 3 (pages 84–86)
Questions 28–40

28 B **29** A **30** C **31** D **32** Y **33** NG **34** Y **35** NG
36 N **37** E **38** A **39** H **40** F

Writing (page 87)

Task 1

Sample answer

Both the bar chart and table give information about
smartphone ownership in 2014. The table shows
differences in the number of people owning a smartphone
in six different countries, while the bar chart focuses
on smartphone ownership in the USA and shows that
smartphones were more popular with younger than older
people.

Looking at the table first, the country with the highest
percentage of smartphone owners was the United Arab
Emirates with 74% of the population. There was a sharp
drop between this country and the next, which was the
USA at 56%. China, South Africa and Russia were at 47%,
40% and 36% respectively, but in India only 13% of people
owned a smartphone, which is the lowest amount shown.

In the bar chart, the highest ownership of smartphones
in the USA was among the 25–34 age group, at 85%,
followed by the 18–24 group at approximately 83%. From
that age to the age of 64, the percentage fell steadily.
Among the over 65s, only 45% owned a smartphone.

Task 2

Sample answer

For some people the idea of becoming famous might
seem like a wonderful ambition, while for others it would
be a major concern. It is clear that there are pros and cons
to both sides, for both society and individuals.

In modern culture, anyone can become famous, often with
no particular skill or talent, and this may seem to have
many advantages for individuals. Celebrities tend to lead
exciting and interesting lives, going to big events and
meeting interesting people. In addition, becoming famous
is associated with making money. Yet many celebrities
find the lifestyle difficult as they lack privacy and have to
endure at times unfair criticism.

As regards society, it could be argued that a culture
in which anyone can be famous is positive in terms of
equality. Even people from poor backgrounds or with few
qualifications have the chance to be successful. However,
this may lead to a society full of role models without skills
or talents, who have not worked hard to achieve success,
but just appeared on a reality TV show. This does not
provide good role models for young people, and will not
motivate them to study and work hard at school.

My own opinion is that the disadvantages of this development outweigh the advantages, because of the potential impact on future generations. Although being famous may be fun for a short time, I believe that for most people it would become difficult and thus it is a negative development for both society and individuals.

Practice Test 4

Listening (pages 89–92)

Section 1 (page 89)

1 solar **2** wood and plastic **3** 1.25 **4** 74 **5** lamp **6** M355X
7 12 month / twelve month / twelve-month **8** 3 August
9 check website **10** £117

Section 2 (page 90)

11 popular **12** beginners **13** Chinese **14** concerts
15 free **16** administrator **17** exams
18 10% / ten percent / ten per cent **19** handbook
20 one week / 1 week / a week

Section 3 (page 91)

21 B **22** A **23** B **24** C **25** A **26** C **27** library
28 torch **29** caves **30** wall

Section 4 (page 92)

31 grandmother **32** café **33** real **34** destroy
35 newspaper **36** wax **37** eye **38** numbers **39** people
40 rare

Reading (pages 93–102)

Reading passage 1 (pages 93–95) Questions 1–13

1 7,522 **2** Yellowstone **3** winds **4** ponderosa
5 Mount Elbert **6** pillars **7** Y **8** NG **9** Y **10** NG **11** N
12 N **13** Y

Reading passage 2 (pages 96–98) Questions 14–27

14 realist / realism **15** (to) art school **16** (an) artists' colony **17** technology **18** light **19** symbolism
20 individuals in society **21** F **22** C **23** D **24** A
25 B **26** B/D **27** B/D

Reading passage 3 (pages 99–102) Questions 28–40

28 B **29** E **30** F **31** D **32** A **33** C **34** G **35** F **36** C
37 A **38** D **39** E **40** B

Writing (page 103)

Task 1

Sample answer

The diagram illustrates how fresh tea is made into tea bags that people buy in supermarkets. Overall, there are six stages shown, beginning with fresh leaves, and ending with a finished tea bag.

To start with, the leaves are placed in a steel drum and blasted with hot air to dry them out. This stage is known as withering. Secondly, the leaves are put on a rotating table to be crushed and torn. Next is the milling stage, when a roller breaks the leaves into smaller pieces, and after that they are sifted through different size sieves. The size of the leaves depends on the type of tea that is being made. They are then mixed together, and flavours added, such as peppermint or ginger. Finally, the tea leaves are measured into piles of 2 grams (grammes) and sealed between two layers of paper to make tea bags.

The end product is packaged for sale.

Task 2

Sample answer

Nowadays, many people have an unhealthy diet and this has led to negative consequences on people's health. Therefore, it could be argued that increasing tax on unhealthy food is a good way to solve this problem. However, there are a range of possible solutions, and this is not the best one in my view.

Putting a high tax on unhealthy food has some advantages. Firstly, there have been previous examples of tax on unhealthy products such as cigarettes and alcohol. Both of these have been highly taxed in the past to prevent people from buying these products. Secondly, it is an easy solution for governments because increasing tax does not cost money, and could actually raise money to pay for healthcare.

On the other hand, raising taxes on unhealthy food has several drawbacks. One issue is the fact that it is unfair to people with a low income, as it will affect them most, and those on higher incomes will continue to buy the food they prefer. Another problem is that it may be complicated to decide which food should be taxed. Should it depend on fat or sugar levels, for example? Furthermore, there are other causes of poor health, such as lack of exercise, as well as unhealthy food.

In conclusion, high tax on unhealthy food seems to be an easy solution to poor diet, but this is simplistic. A better idea would be to make fruit, vegetables and other healthy food cheaper, by subsidising the cost. This would be fairer, and a positive step rather than a negative one.

Author: Liz Joiner (Listening, Writing and Speaking: Practice Tests and Boost Your Score lessons)

Additional material: Fiona Davis (Reading: Boost Your Score lessons)

Publisher: Gordon Knowles

Senior Development Editor: Fiona Davis

Design: Oxford Designers & Illustrators Ltd

Cover design: Nicolle Thomas

Picture research: Suzanne Williams

Picture credits:

Page 7: L.Steward/iStockphoto; Chesnot/Getty Images.

Page 8: I.Bondarenko/iStockphoto.

Page 11: CBCK-Christine/iStockphoto.

Page 14: shapecharge/iStockphoto.

Page 37: saiko3p/iStockphoto.

Page 53: g-stockstudio/iStockphoto.

Page 64: maki_shmaki/iStockphoto.

Page 76: AustralianCamera/iStockphoto.

Page 93: traveler1116/iStockphoto.

The publishers are grateful for permission to reproduce and adapt the following copyright material:

All articles from The Independent are reproduced with permission from The Independent.

'The Green Hay-Fever Machine' (Steve Connor, 18th October, 2011) © The Independent; 'Get ready for the sneezing season' (Fiona Roberts, 4th May, 2010) © The Independent; 'Car ownership in households in England and Wales 2001 and 2011' Data source: 2011 Census – Key Statistics for England and Wales, March 2011: 14 Car or van availability. Office for National Statistics 2012; 'Number of adults who played sports once a week in England in 2005–2006 and 2015–2016' Data source: Sport England Active People Survey 10Q2 April 2015 – March 2016 © Sport England; 'The History of Jenolan Caves' Reproduced with permission from the Jenolan Caves Reserve Trust; 'The Big Question: What does forward-planning reveal about chimps' relationship to humans?' (Steve Connor, 11th March, 2009) © The Independent; 'Flaming 2008 by Zevs Dirty City Wall, Copenhagen' (Michael Glover, 29th December 2012) © The Independent; 'Total money spent online in the USA' Reproduced with permission from Statista; 'Proportion of total purchases made online in one company in the USA' © Market Realist; 'Indian palaces' (Aoife O'Riordain 2nd January, 2010) © The Independent; 'Out of Africa: stone tools rewrite history

of man as a global species' (Steve Connor, 28th January, 2011) © The Independent; 'The smelling test' (Laura Spinney, 24th January 2011) © The Independent; 'Georgia O'Keeffe: An extraordinary show long overdue' (Karen Wright, 6th July 2016) © The Independent; How a wind turbine works Data source: Edge FX (http://efxkits.com/blog/working-of-solar-wind-hybrid-system); 'In it for the honey' (Christopher Hirst, 30th October, 2010) © The Independent; 'The Flight of the Commodore' (Rhodri Marsden, 26th January, 2012) © The Independent'; 'The truth about Melville remains as elusive as that great white whale' (David Evans, 16th January, 2011)© The Independent; 'U.S. smartphone owners by age group' Data source: Nielsen, 2014; 'Colorado Rockies: At the great divide' (Steve Connor, 16th July, 2011) © The Independent; 'By the end of the century half of all species will be extinct. Does that matter?' (Julia Whitty, 30th April 2007) © The Independent; 'Manufacture of a teabag' Data source: Advameg, Inc (http://www.madehow.com/Volume-2/Tea-bag.html)

The publishers are grateful for permission from Scholastic Inc., for use of the following articles and data:

'Spotlight: Anish Kapoor' (ART Magazine, April/May 2015); 'Click-to-gift' (Scholastic Math magazine, November 17, 2014); 'Keeping Their Cool' (Science World, November 17, 2014); 'Help! I can't put down my phone' (Choices, May 2016); 'Devils Fight Back' (Science World, February 13, 2017); 'Rise of the Smartphone' (Scholastic Math magazine, January 12, 2015); 'Spotlight: Jasper Johns' (ART Magazine, March 2015); 'Spotlight: Edward Hopper' (ART Magazine, December, 2016)

Printed in the UK by Bell and Bain Ltd, Glasgow

ISBN: 9781407169712